To Die Is Gain

And Other
Suicidal Thoughts

A Memoir Of Drawing Closer To Christ
In Life, Crisis, And Recovery

Alison Olson

Printed in the United States of America
First Printing 2019
First Edition 2019
ISBN: 978-1-7331725-0-9

10 9 8 7 6 5 4 3 2 1

To Die Is Gain
And Other
Suicidal Thoughts

TABLE OF CONTENTS

INTRODUCTION

"Write what disturbs you, what you fear, what you have not been willing to speak about." —Natalie Goldberg, *Writing Down the Bones*

A young coworker committed suicide in 2015, leaving behind two small children. Social media swarmed with the buzzing of the news. She had left a suicide note of sorts as a post. It took many by surprise, but for some, they knew beforehand. From the Facebook comments, you could hear the guilt, the astonishment, and even the anger in the tone of their words. Some comments were mean and hurtful, and they angered me. I had thoughts of suicide before, so I could empathize with this poor woman's desperation.

I authored a comment but lacked the courage to post it. Instead, I sent it to my best friend and asked for her thoughts. Here it is.

"Geez, we are human; give us a break. If I hear one more person say that suicide is selfish, I may vomit right on them. It's not selfish; it's a sickness. How sad are the lives that they cannot see out of their darkness? The tunnel has closed in and they know not a way out nor any hope of it getting better. There is a great courage in the act of passing into the unknown! And there is selflessness in leaving a world they believe to be better off without them, but we don't see that! It is sick, yes, but it's not selfish. Selfish is thinking that you had anything to do with the decision. In their sickness, they didn't even see you. So please stop trying to understand and just show compassion for those in pain. Hurtful words won't help the healing."

My friend told me not to post it. Her main issue was she didn't agree with it. It would be adding fuel to the fire and sparking additional and unnecessary, debate. Reading this comment scared me. These were my thoughts and feelings on suicide that had been planted in my heart over time. I didn't realize how they would grow.

PART ONE

Perspective is everything... Every single day, someone is having the best day ever. And every single day, someone is having the worst day ever. Everyone else is just living in between those two days.

Both good things and bad things happen to everyone sooner or later, but whatever happens is God's will. So, live in gratitude no matter what. Know God's truth and strength will guide you through *any* day.

Any day now could be your best day. Any day now could be your worst. But, EVERY day, you are blessed.

Introduction

CHAPTER 1:
CHECKBOX CHRISTIAN

Demographically, I am a Christian. That is, if you were to give me a form to fill out asking for my demographic information, I would check female, white, non-Hispanic, and Christian - Protestant or otherwise. I don't hang it like a banner outside or possess memorabilia like a favorite sports team. Truly, I thought if God could see my heart, he would know I did enough to meet the definition.

Are you religious? No, but I am spiritual. Where do you worship? Well, um, maybe singing in the car to Christian radio or at home with a devotional. My relationship with God was personal, and I didn't share it. I didn't want to flaunt it or make it appear like something it wasn't.

It turns out there wasn't much to talk about anyway. In fear of going against the grain or misrepresenting the faith, I chose not to label myself publicly as a Christian. I wasn't a good example and didn't want someone to judge the faith by my inability to model it appropriately.

Religious debates that time to time rose up I would avoid. Christians are hypocrites, right? I get the perception. It would seem, looking back, ceasing to talk out loud *about* God also hinders your desire to talk *to* God. In fact, the hardest times in my adult life were when I was the furthest away from Him.

A faith-eating tumor is planted inside of me, figuratively that is. It's an ugly black mass of depression, hate, fear, anger, resentment, and discontent. Reading the Bible, participating in Bible studies, attending adult Sunday school, and going to church are like treatments. Over time, if I stay consistent, the tumor gets smaller. The space in my soul frees up then fills with love, understanding, peace, and hope.

Unfortunately, I feel today as if my condition is incurable. Just when I start to feel better, the dark mass grows back. Sometimes, it even gets as big or bigger then when I first started this journey. The darkness is suffocating and terribly uncomfortable. So much so, I have wanted to end this journey of life altogether.

I don't like thinking about suicide, but it happens. It can get scary, and I don't trust myself at times. I got rid of my gun several years ago after a close call. I knew better than to keep the bullets close by. Extra pills get flushed, but car trips are inescapable. I would never go left of center toward another car, but off the side into something hard and cheap I have considered.

What keeps me from going through with it? Honestly, failure. I have looked into the eyes of the man, lying in the emergency room, who awakens after an overdose and have seen the disappointment on his face. Additionally, I want to know what I am getting myself into. What is waiting for me after death? How many times do you hear, "Well, it can't get any worse" only to see life turn in exactly that direction?

I lost my dad after a horrific vehicle crash resulting in a traumatic brain injury. Three years later when his body gave up completely, I lost him again to death. Shortly after, my husband and I got a divorce. I didn't think it could get any worse. Little did I know, it was only the beginning.

My mother remarried and so did I. I didn't like my stepdad at first, but I grew to respect and care for him very much. My brother got married and had a little boy. There was the birth of both of my beautiful sons, so it wasn't all bad. I am blessed beyond measure for having them. Those little boys are my reason for living.

Nevertheless, pregnancy was hard. Marriage was hard. Living without my dad around was hard. Taking care of my husband's demented grandmother was hard. Dealing with my husband's alcoholic parents was hard. Moving to a different house every year for seven years was hard. Switching jobs was hard. Watching my aunt suffer from a spinal cord injury was hard. Seeing my father's family fall apart was hard. Keeping friends was hard.

Just when I thought it was too hard, it got worse. When my second marriage fell apart, it was worse. When I moved out of a house I shared with my kids, it was worse. When my husband announced his engagement and pregnancy with a woman from work prior to our divorce, it was worse. When my mother was diagnosed with stage four liver cancer, it was worse. When my stepdad died suddenly of a heart attack, it was worse. When I was passed over for a promotion at work to an incompetent self-righteous, asshat it was worse. (I'm not bitter; can you tell?) Betrayed and humiliated by those whom I thought at least cared was worse. Moving to a town I didn't want to be in and leaving a job I loved was worse. Trying to deal with all of this on my own without acknowledging and giving thanks and praise for the unconditional love and support of Jesus Christ was the worst.

My adult life, by and large, has been a saga of heartbreak. I'm on a journey now of redemption. There has got to be more to this life than loss. His plan for me has to be more than survival. What do I have left to lose? It can't get any worse...

Chapter 1: Checkbox Christian

Chapter 2:
Grateful... Kind Of

It's a new year and it started like most of the years of my adult life… bad. My kids were terribly sick and then I got terribly sick. My husband and I got into a fight over healthcare stuff for the boys. My mom continues to struggle with chemo treatments every week.

Oh, wait; sorry, I'm trying to be more grateful, so let's see. I am thankful for my job, and it's getting better each day as my interest grows in the medical field. My youngest son has autism spectrum disorder and is primarily nonverbal. He got a push-button speech-generating device this week, so the possibility of giving him a voice is exciting. I appreciate deeply the honesty and support my brother gives me as we wade through the uncertain waters of family matters.

Do you know I have had more parents die and suffer from disease now than grandparents? That just seems like it shouldn't be. I had one grandmother pass when I was a junior in high school. I remember being at the hospital the day she died. All the family were waiting in line to say their good-byes, but I heard what was going to happen and disappeared. I didn't want to see her on her death bed. I didn't want that image burned into my mind. I loved her very much and am thankful to this day that I didn't go in there. She knew I loved her. I didn't need to remind her once again. And I knew she loved me, because I was her favorite, the baby girl.

I was there, bedside, when my father passed away. I hate that day and hate that memory. The sound, the smell, the look of panic on his face was horrible as he essentially was allowed to suffocate. I get it. He was sick, he had been sick for a couple years. We had many scares, but he was a survivor. Trauma to the brain is very tricky. It impacts the body in the strangest of ways.

Do you know how important it is to swallow? It's an instinct, an ability you never had to learn. But what if that part of your brain was damaged and you forgot. Imagine if you had to learn it over again and then remember to keep doing it. Then imagine if your memory was impaired as well. You would forget to swallow; you would choke on your own saliva. After everything he had survived, to try and understand that his own spit was what finally did him in was so hard to comprehend. He was in a crushing car accident and survived with a heart beating as strong as ever. He spent three years in rehabilitation fighting to get home. One night he forgot to swallow and his need to breathe overcame him. He aspirated, got pneumonia, and died.

My stepdad had a bad ticker from jumpstart. When he met my mom, he was a smoker and already survived one heart attack. I knew my mom adored him and he would do a good job taking care of her, but I didn't know if he knew what he was getting into. Our family is not an easy one. There were moments I didn't think they would make it. I fought to support them as best I could because my mom deserved to be happy. She had already lost her high school sweetheart.

After mom was diagnosed with cancer, all eyes were on her. We all loved her and cared for her. She was the glue that bound us. In hindsight, I should have looked after him more. He started overeating, smoking more, and was diagnosed with diabetes. His heart was hurting in every way. The call came early in the morning and we rushed to the hospital. His heart stopped completely when in the examination room, and they couldn't revive him.

Context is important to understand. My mom's first husband was dealt a hand, did the best he could, and eventually failed. There was a sense of relief that lives next to our grief. That guilt is hard to deal with, but we knew his quality of life wasn't great. We learned the hard lesson that there are fates worse than death. My mom's second husband was her emancipation. But then, when she was in her hour of need, sick, cancer-ridden, weak, and hairless, he was taken like a theft in the night. The shock of grief took the breath right out of you. "What am I going to do?" she cried. I remember the pain in her voice and twisted agony on her face as if it were yesterday.

Now my mom fights for her life every week. Chemo has been ongoing for 18 months now. I don't know how much more her body can take. She sleeps most of the time and her body hurts day and night. She struggles to renew each week what the chemo kills. Worse of all for me, she can't see the reality of her illness. I know her everlasting faith and hope that God will save her is inspiring. She inspired me long before she had cancer and the good Lord has saved her life every day for the last 18 months. Every doctor has told us she shouldn't have lived this long. So, I get it, but, like I said before, there are worse fates than death and people live them every day.

She will only get worse. The cancer is incurable. She can fight like mad, but she won't win. She can't work as treatment is her job. She sleeps more than she is awake. She's aging quickly. Mom chose this life of being a pharmaceutical guinea pig. It breaks my heart to watch, but I must respect her choice. Doing nothing, she says, is giving up, and we don't give up.

If she would only quit chemo, she would feel so amazing. She could enjoy her time and be awake for it. She could renew and feel alive again. The color would come back to her face and the light brighter in her eyes. But she won't quit, so I fear I may never see her well again.

She is a prayer warrior. Every morning, she goes to her "war room" and prays. Well or not, she prays. If she prays for healing, I pray she sees God has already done this. If she prays for strength, I pray she sees God has already provided this. If she prays for one more day, I pray she sees God has already granted this. God has already answered her prayers and ours. We are grateful. She will not survive this, but that's okay. God does understand, God provides, and God answers. God will take care of her as he did yesterday, does today, and will forevermore.

So, that didn't sound terribly grateful. Sounded more like a sob story. Ugh, this is hard. With so much pain and suffering, it's hard to look for the good and what we have to be thankful for. I know it's not much, but, truly, it took me months to get to this place of gratitude. Specifically, it took antidepressants, weeks of therapy, sometimes healthier food choices, Bible studies, and daily spiritual attendance. It's not easy, but I'm in a better place. I know God is always there, but, still, I don't talk to him much. I should pray more and with a thankful heart. I am thankful my birthday is just around the corner!

CHAPTER 3:
IT'S ALL ABOUT ME... I MEAN YOU

I'm a big birthday fan and an even bigger fan of my own birthday. For most of my 20s, I tried and tried to get folks to catch on to half birthdays. Other than my bestie, no one took the bait. The year going into my 30th birthday I changed strategies. I started a countdown. Each year would have a theme and I would only countdown as many days as I was going to be in age. So, with 30 days until my 30th birthday, the countdown was born!

Gratefulness was my first theme. Everyday for 30 days I posted on Facebook something I was thankful for from snow days to motherhood to my lovely upbringing. I had no trouble coming up with posts as God has blessed me in many ways. (See, I really can be positive.)

With 31 days until my 31st birthday, I initiated the kindness countdown. Everyday for 31 days I performed a random act of kindness. This adventure certainly raised the bar. I planned and researched and laid the groundwork. I bought a single mother breakfast, left a baggie of quarters at the laundry mat, and carried an elderly woman's grocery sacks out to her car. It was a good birthday countdown and very fulfilling.

For my 32nd birthday, it was all about pictures. Blast from the past countdown featured wonderful memories captured in photos. It was fun and so many followers as more and more folks became included and featured as well. Permed hair, prom dresses, family vacations, and baby pictures it was fun for all.

This year, I turn 33. To be honest, it was hard getting excited about 33. After new years, I started thinking about what theme the countdown should be this year. I had really started to focus more on my faith, so brainstormed ways of including it in some way. (look here I even see what the problem is, including faith in my life? It shouldn't be a piece of life it is life... sorry back to me, I mean you... well, just stay tuned)

Facebook and social media in general were full of despair after a difficult political election season. Inspiration was hard to find. After little progress, I decided that I should try to practice what has been preached and pray about it. So, I asked God to guide me. I started looking anxiously for his answer instead of waiting for it. I could do my 33 favorite Christian songs, 33 memory verses, or 33 fun Bible facts. Is this the answer? I asked Him, raising my eyes to the sky and listening intently. I heard nothing but crickets.

I counted out the days and set a reminder on my phone. Something would surely provide inspiration by then. The morning the countdown was to begin, I felt lost and unanswered. My Bible was staring at me. I reached over and open it up and started reading aimlessly. The great "I am" had answered my prayer. I researched all day.

There are so many different names used for God including the well-known "I am". The list is extraordinary including Lord, Creator, Redeemer, King, Judge, Deliverer, Savior, Shepherd, and Rock. There is no doubt He is almighty and wonderful. Even more amazing is He, who is above all things, adores *me*. He is my biggest fan and loves me unconditionally. It's still a wonder why this is, but the Bible was clear, God says you and I are awesome.

What did the great "I am" think about us? I turned the question around and found a new perspective. Instead of searching for "I am" I looked at "you are". Searching my Bible app, the idea blossomed. You are a masterpiece. You are sacred. You are blessed. Each finding was more and more encouraging. That was it! "You are" encouragement countdown was to be the theme. When listening for God's answer, it can be helpful to hear his word.

That day I charted 15 different verses that revealed exactly how amazing God says we are. Every day, I've been faithfully posting a "you are" statement, Bible verse to support, and a Pinterest picture for visual effect. I also promised to only post my countdown, no shares, no some-ecards, no selfies, and no negativity. Instead, I focused on others. I responded with kind words, liked, loved, and laughed at their posts. With some, I grieved. I found several new Facebook pages to follow, which post Christian words of encouragement and love.

The first two days were good. I had almost 30 likes. I made sure the posts were public instead of just for my friends. I was excited to share these encouraging words with everyone. I dreamed the countdown would go viral and numerous followers would start checking in daily to see what the next message was about. This was far from reality. Ten days into the countdown I was more discouraged than encouraged. At maximum, I had 15 likes. Most days there were only 6. My friends are further from the Lord than I thought. Several of my friends and family members haven't liked one post, not one. It really has me questioning the type of people I have chosen to be a part of my life. Maybe their presence in my life is more of secular negativity.

I prayed and searched for deeper understanding. "You are" research continued using my Bible app, Pinterest, and Christian Facebook groups I had started following. I had outlined 22 posts up to this point and only 11 to go. Then I realized something very important. God was filling my mind full of love in new ways.

In my search to encourage others using "You are" Bible references, I changed the way I sought out information. Today, when I pull up Facebook, I see encouraging posts from Christian group pages and get notification of new encouraging words. I open Pinterest and there are dozens of positive quotes and Biblical references under the "you may like" section. I have read scriptures from my Bible app everyday. God has changed my world.

We forget how influential we are in this age of technology. Its consumer driven, but we forget our hands are on the wheel. You get out what you put in right? That's basically the algorithm or binary code or whatever. It is so easy to get stuck in "shock and awe" land where the outrageous and unbelievable rule. Just taking the last 22 days and mindfully searching for the good and uplifting has changed my journey altogether.

CHAPTER 4:
"YOU ARE" POWERFUL

This was a great Bible study and devotional experience for me. I would encourage you to spend some time on each one. Maybe you can do your own 33-day countdown or Bible study. I pray you can internalize the message and believe the truth that God loves you, trusts you, and values you.

33RD BIRTHDAY COUNTDOWN

33   Jan 14

33rd Birthday Countdown: 33 days until my 33rd birthday! I have to tell you that I am kind of a big deal. But guess what? So are you! My countdown this year is one of encouragement. "You Are" is the theme and I intend to show you, through God's word, how amazing you are. He is the great "I am" and YOU ARE great because you are His.
Matthew 5:14-16
You are the light of the world. A town built on a hill cannot be hidden. Neither do people light a lamp and put it under a bowl. Instead they put it on its stand, and it gives light to everyone in the house. In the same way, let your light shine before others, that they may see your good deeds and glorify your Father in heaven.

32   Jan 15

YOU ARE a masterpiece. God designed you deliberately long before your existence.
Psalm 139:13-14,16

For you created my inmost being; you knit me together in my mother's womb. I praise you because I am fearfully and wonderfully made; your works are wonderful, I know that full well. Your eyes saw my unformed body; all the days ordained for me were written in your book before one of them came to be.

31   Jan 16

YOU ARE strong. There is nothing to fear as He will sustain you.
Isaiah 41:9-10
I took you from the ends of the earth, from its farthest corners I called you. I said, 'You are my servant'; I have chosen you and have not rejected you. So do not fear, for I am with you; do not be dismayed, for I am your God. I will strengthen you and help you. I will uphold you with my righteous right hand.

30   Jan 17

YOU ARE equal. No one is above you or below you when you are all one in Christ.
Galatians 3:26-28
So, in Christ Jesus you are all children of God through faith, for all of you who were baptized into Christ have clothes yourselves with Christ. There is neither Jew nor Gentile, neither slave nor free, nor is there male and female, for you are all one in Christ Jesus.

29   Jan 18

YOU ARE never alone. His goodness and love are with you always.
Psalm 23:4-6
Even though I walk through the darkest valley, you are with me; your rod and your staff they comfort me. You prepare a table before me in the presence of my enemies. You anoint my head with oil; my cup overflows. Surely your goodness and love will follow me all the days of my life, and I will dwell in the house of the Lord forever.

28   Jan 19

YOU ARE safe. He will deliver you and surround you in His unfailing love.
Psalm 32:7,10-11
You are my hiding place; you will protect me from trouble and surround me with songs of deliverance. Many are the woes of the wicked, but the Lord's unfailing love surrounds the one who trusts in him. Rejoice in the Lord and be glad, you righteous; sing, all you who are upright in heart!

27   Jan 20

YOU ARE sacred. Your body is a holy and blessed gift.
1Corithians 6:18-20
All other sins a person commits are outside the body, but whoever sins sexually, sins against their own body. Do you not know that your bodies are temples of the Holy Spirit, who is in you, whom you have received from God? You are not your own; you were bought at a price. Therefore honor God with your bodies.

26   Jan 21

YOU ARE fruitful. The Spirit of God is inside you and will produce wonders in your life.
Galatians 5:22
But the fruit of the Spirit is love, joy, peace, patience, kindness, goodness, faithfulness, gentleness, self-control; against such things there is no law. And those who belong to Christ Jesus have crucified the flesh with its passions and desires. If we live by the Spirit, let us also keep in step with the Spirit.

25   Jan 22

YOU ARE enlightened. Christ's radiance shining on your face and in your heart can brighten any day.
Ephesians 5:8-11,13

For you were once darkness, but now you are light in the Lord. Live as children of light (for the fruit of the light consists in all goodness, righteousness, and truth) and find out what pleases the Lord. Have nothing to do with the fruitless deeds of darkness, but rather expose them... everything exposed by the light becomes visible- and everything that is illuminated becomes a light.

24   Jan 23

YOU ARE protected. He holds you and keeps you in His unfailing love.
Psalm 31:3-5
Since you are my rock and my fortress, for the sake of your name lead and guide me. Keep me free from the trap that is set for me, for you are my refuge. Into your hand I commit my spirit; deliver me, Lord, my faithful God.

23   Jan 24

YOU ARE privileged. You are a member of God's household, a shelter unlike any other.
Ephesians 2:19-22
You are no longer foreigners and strangers, but fellow citizens with God's people and also members of his household, built on the foundations of the apostles and prophets, with Christ Jesus himself as the chief cornerstone. In him the whole building is joined together and rises to become a holy temple in the Lord. And in him you too are being built together to become a dwelling in which God lives by his Spirit.

22   Jan 25

YOU ARE a child of God. You will always have a family.
Romans 8:14-16
For those who are led by the Spirit of God are the children of God. The Spirit you received does not make you slaves, so that you live in fear again; rather, the Spirit you received brought about your adoption to sonship.

And by him we cry, "Abba, Father." The Spirit himself testifies with our spirit that we are God's children.

21   Jan 26

YOU ARE royal. As a child of the King, you are magnificent.
Romans 8:17
Now if we are children, then we are heirs- heirs of God and co-heirs with Christ, if indeed we share in his sufferings in order that we may also share in his glory.
2Titus 2:11-12
If we died with him, we will also live with him; if we endure, we will also reign with him.

20   Jan 27

YOU ARE part of Christ's body. Whether you are hands, feet, liver, or funny bone, you are a special and important part.
I Corinthians 12:12,24-27
Just as a body, though one, has many parts, but all its many parts form one body, so it is with Christ… God has put the body together…so that there should be no division in the body, but that its parts should have equal concern for each other. If one part suffers, every part suffers with it; if one part is honored, every part rejoices with it. No you are the body of Christ, and each one of you is a part of it.

19   Jan 28

YOU ARE loved. He has saved you.
Psalm 86:12-13
I will praise you, Lord my God, with all my heart; I will glorify your name forever. For great is your love toward me; you have delivered me from the depths, from the realm of the dead.

18   Jan 29

YOU ARE free. You are not a slave to this world.

2 Corinthians 3:17

Now the Lord is the Spirit, and where the Spirit of the Lord is, there is freedom.

17   Jan 30

YOU ARE cared for. He will provide for you, so believe and trust your Father will give you what you need.

1 Peter5:7

Cast all your anxiety on him because he cares for you.

Psalm 55:22

Cast your cares on the Lord and he will sustain you; he will never let the righteous be shaken.

16   Jan 31

YOU ARE worth fighting for. Put your gloves down and give it to God.

Exodus 14:14

The Lord will fight for you; you need only to be still.

Deuteronomy 3:22

Do not be afraid of them; the Lord your God himself will fight for you.

Deuteronomy 20:4

For the Lord your God is the one who goes with you to fight for you against your enemies to give you victory.

15   Feb 1

YOU ARE blessed. Our Father's blessings never cease and his mercies are new day after day after day.

Matthew 5:3-12

Blessed are the poor in spirit, for theirs is the kingdom of heaven.

Blessed are those who mourn for they will be comforted.

Blessed are the meek, for they will inherit the earth.

Blessed are those who hunger and thirst for righteousness, for they will be filled.

Blessed are the merciful, for they will be shown mercy.

Blessed are the pure in heart, for they will see God.

Blessed are the peacemakers, for they will be called children of God.

Blessed are those who are persecuted because of righteousness, for theirs is the kingdom of heaven.

Blessed are you when people insult you, persecute you and falsely say all kinds of evil against you because of me. Rejoice and be glad, because great is your reward in heaven.

14   Feb 2

YOU ARE defended. There is so much evil, pain, and injustices in this world. Care not what other's think of you as His opinion is the only one that decides your eternity and can heal your brokenness.

2 Thessalonians 1:5-7

God's judgment is right, and as a result you will be counted worthy of the kingdom of God, for which you are suffering. God is just: He will pay back trouble to those who trouble you and give relief to you who are troubled, and to us as well.

13   Feb 3

YOU ARE a friend of Christ. There is no better BFF than Jesus. He is the perfect comrade whom you can trust always.

John 15:13-14

Greater Love has no one than this: to lay down one's life for one's friends. You are my friends if you do what I command.

12   Feb 4

YOU ARE made new. There is so much this world has done to break us, hurt us, and tear us away from Jesus. It can leave us bitter and cold. But you are not of this world, the Spirit of the Lord lives in you and can renew your heart in Christ.

Ezekiel 36:26-28

I will give you a new heart and put a new spirit in you; I will remove form you your heart of stone and give you a heart of flesh. And I will put my Spirit in you and move you to follow my decrees and be careful to keep my laws. Then you will live in the land I gave your ancestors; you will be my people, and I will be your God.

11   Feb 5

YOU ARE good. There is a difference between acting foolish and being a fool. You may do bad things, but you are not a bad person. God knew what wonderful things you would do from the beginning, so fill your heart with encouragement as his goodness is already there.

Ephesians 2:10

For we are God's handiwork, created in Christ Jesus to do good works, which God prepared in advance for us to do.

10   Feb 6

YOU ARE created for a purpose. You are not a "filler" for the earth's population. You are not a mistake. God has big plans for you!

Jeremiah 29:11

"For I know the plans I have for you," declares the Lord, "plans to prosper you and not to harm you, plans to give you hope and a future."

9   Feb 7

YOU ARE transformed. Change your thoughts and you can change your life. Feed your mind with His word and it will consume your heart.

Romans 12:2

Do not conform to the pattern of this world, but be transformed by the renewing of your mind. Then you will be able to test and approve what God's will is – his good, pleasing and perfect will.

8   Feb 8

YOU ARE chosen. You are never left out or left behind. God's love is all-inclusive.

1 Peter 2:9-10

But you are a chosen people, a royal priesthood, a holy nation, God's special possession, that you may declare the praises of him who called you out of darkness into his wonderful light. Once you were not a people, but now you are the people of God; once you had not received mercy, but now you have received mercy.

7   Feb 9

YOU ARE forgiven. Guilt is a horrible feeling and can overcome your feelings of self-worth. How can God love you after you've done such terrible things? He does and you must accept His endless grace. He loves you and forgives you.

Psalm 103:8,10,12

The Lord is compassionate and gracious, slow to anger, abounding in love... he does not treat us as our sins deserve or repay us according to our iniquities... as far as the east is from the west, so far has he removed our transgressions from us.

6   Feb 10

YOU ARE empowered. His strength is with you whether you are climbing mountains or struggling to stay afloat. In any situation, God will give you strength.

Philippians 4:12-13

I know what it is to be in need, for I have learned to be content whatever the circumstances. I know what it is to be in need, and I know what it is to have plenty. I have learned the secret of being content in any and every situation, whether well fed or hungry, whether living in plenty or in want. I can do all this through him who gives me strength.

5   Feb 11

YOU ARE redeemed. God does not ration forgiveness. It is poured out on us. God's grace is like drinking water from a fire hydrant. You can take in all you can, and he offers so much more.

Ephesians 1:7-8
In him, we have redemption through his blood, the forgiveness of sins, in accordance with the riches of God's grace that he lavished on us.

4   Feb 12

YOU ARE favored. It is the greatest honor of your life on earth to glorify God. Listen, watch, and wait.
Proverbs 8:34-35
Blessed are those who listen to me, watching daily at my doors, waiting at my doorway. For those who find me find life and receive favor from the Lord.

3   Feb 13

YOU ARE under God's care. The one who made you and loves you will take care of you always.
Psalm 95:6-7
Come, let us bow down in worship, let us kneel before the Lord our Maker; for he is our God and we are the people of his pasture, the flock under his care.

2   Feb 14

YOU ARE healed. He took your suffering, your wickedness, and your injustice. Let Him take the pain, as it's not yours to bear anymore.
Isaiah 53:5
He was pierced for our transgressions, he was crushed for our iniquities; the punishment that brought us peace was on him, and by his wounds we are healed.

1   Feb 15

YOU ARE saved. Believe in Jesus and what he has already done for you and you will be saved.

Romans 10:9-13

If you declare with your mouth, "Jesus is Lord," and believe in your heart that God raised him from the dead, you will be saved. For it is with your heart that you believe and are justified, and it is with your mouth that you profess your faith and are saved. As Scripture says, "Anyone who believes in him will never be put to shame," For there is no difference between Jew and Gentile – the same Lord is Lord of all and richly blesses all who call on him, for, "everyone who calls on the name of the Lord will be saved."

0   February 16, 2017 Happy Birthday to ME!

CHAPTER 4: "YOU ARE" POWERFUL

CHAPTER 5:
SHOW ME THE ~~MONEY~~ WAY

I approached God about my finances much like I had involved Him in other areas of my life… half-way. After my second divorce (a saga for another day), I was in debt up to my eyeballs. Actually, worse than that, it was more like my head was below water and I had a small bendy straw just above the surface.

Finances were of grave debate in both marriages. The first one was a disaster. To this day, I know little of the details, but the punch line is this… He had a bookie and in one boxing match, it was all gone. The exact number I never knew, but it was over $100,000. I didn't even know about the account or the gambling until it came crashing to a halt. We moved forward until I found a list of college football games for that Saturday complete with winners and point differences. It was the beginning of the end.

The second marriage was a bit more hopeful. He worked two jobs most the time. If we needed more money, he would pick up a shift. If we wanted something, it was bought on credit. Big screen TVs, vacations, and so much more. We didn't save a dime. We had two mortgages and 163 acres of hunting land, but no liquid assets. It was so easy, but then again, we were living month to month and not growing any wealth. It was just one piece of the puzzle that lead to our demise, but a significant one.

Divorce left me with two mortgages (both in my name due to his bad credit), a car payment (should have been paid off but had been refinanced), and about $15,000 in credit card debt. I didn't have a clue what to do. As a social worker, I would have referred a client in similar straits to housing and credit counseling, so that's what I did. The appointment was fairly harmless, and the counselor was gentle and fair. My options were bleak. File for bankruptcy or take drastic measures to cut costs. The first to go, she suggested, was my charitable donations. I just couldn't.

Bankruptcy was taboo and would certainly bring dishonor on me and my family. What would my grandparents think? You pay what you owe, so I had to figure it out. I knew little about finances and budgeting, so I went to the house of knowledge, the library. After searching a while, I ran into a popular book called *The Total Money Makeover* by Dave Ramsey. I had heard about this guy and knew he had a radio show. It was supposed to be all about managing money as a Christian. It was worth a shot. They offered it in audio book format too, even better.

I took it home and put it in my CD player. I listened intently and took notes. Quickly overwhelmed, I only made it to baby step number two, but it was enough. Step 1 was to save $1,000. Done and actually to my own surprise I had a little more than that in savings. Step 2 was the debt snowball. Dave said starting with the smallest balance pay off your debt. Credit card A with $500 credit limit, bam! paid off. Next was credit card B with $1500 balance, so I paid a good chunk on it. Now I'd take the monthly payment I was paying on credit card A, I just paid off, and add it to the monthly payment I have on the remainder of credit card B to get it paid off faster. Once credit card B was paid off then on to the next. Now to pay off credit card C with a balance of $3000, I had the monthly payments of credit cards A and B to add to credit card C monthly payment. And so, the debt snowball grew.

Not only did I pay off debt, but I had to agree to stop adding debt. So, I had to watch my expenditures more carefully since my credit cards were not available to "supplement" my income. The audio book in Dave's enthusiastic voice encourages me to go after my debt with "gazelle like intensity." "Run for your life!" he says. Use everything you can to get it paid off. I used my tax refund, sold my extra "stuff" at a garage sale, cancelled cable and Internet, pawned jewelry I never wore, cashed out my IRA (after all I'm only 32 and have time to save even more).

It was only about 18 months after my divorce, and I was out of credit card debt! Living in the black and not the red was making all the difference. I cannot say that some blunders and absurdities didn't creep in, as they certainly did. And there was definitely more than one set back. But I had done it!

However, I was only on step 2, and I lost my intensity. I never went back to the book to see what I was supposed to do next. I got a new job and was making more money. The use of credit cards was no longer an issue. I had even saved back about $2,000. Budgeting was no longer a habit, so finances became a lost thought.

My paid-off SUV broke down, and I used the $2,000 in savings to buy a new car. A $254 monthly payment was added. Internet was the reward I gave myself for paying off credit card debt, so another $60 a month was added as well. Entertainment was quite diverting, so extra cash went to purchasing tickets to the ballet, comedy club, musicals, and Disney live with the kiddos. I showered my sons with new toys and gadgets. We went to numerous outings and bought all kinds of memorabilia. Before I knew it, I was back in the red.

You know what? I missed the whole point. I get that hindsight is 20/20. But, how could I have forgotten the most important part of it all? I ran toward the goal with gazelle like intensity, but I left God behind. He wasn't a part of my plans for success which really was no plan at all.

My God is so good to me. Mercifully, he gave me another chance to get it right. The church bulletin one Sunday late last year announced a new class offering Financial Peace University: Dave Ramsey's Complete Guide to Money. I signed up quickly and had my spot secured. I prayed for discipline to find me come the new year. For now, its back to work, work, work.

CHAPTER 6:
IT'S A BOY

What an incredibly emotionally conflicting day! It was a long day, much longer that I had ever anticipated and full of anguish and beauty. My good friend and coworker was out of town on holiday, so I was covering her unit. I don't think we've discussed this yet, but I'm a social worker at a hospital.

I usually cover the progressive care unit (full of patients with strokes and hospice cases) and the inpatient rehab unit (still full of patient with strokes, but also Parkinson's and other debilitating and often life-changing diseases). I do good work in my departments and can handle the cases quite well. I have adapted to the ever-changing human condition and the complex family systems they often come giftwrapped in. Dead bodies, with either grieving loved ones or empty chairs at their bedsides, I have strategized emotionally and coped with effectively thus far.

Today, I covered the new life center. Labor and delivery was on one side of the hallway with postpartum beds on the other. My day was forlorn as soon as I opened the inbox. Not one or two, but three cases of mothers with newborns who tested positive for illegal substances. Another case of a mother in a relationship scarred with domestic violence. I had expected maybe three or four educational counseling sessions on community resources, but only one today.

My phone rang, it was the nurses' station, so let the fun begin. "We need you today," she said. I'm starting chart reviews now and will be on my way. Chart reviews for three units took until 10am. I triaged the progressive care unit in one hour and put the inpatient rehab admits on the back burner, they'll be there tomorrow. By 11:30am, I was knee deep wading through the series of social dramas that could easily be made into a Lifetime Movie.

Forgive my brutal descriptions, but it wasn't the lying pot-head mom or minimizing punching-bag mom who bothered me so much. It was meth mom who is tugging at my feelers right now. I had dealt with her "type" for years, so why was this hard? Addiction is an evil like no other. I used to think maternal love was one of the most powerful things on earth, but I've seen addiction win over this seemingly unbreakable bond. I've watched as mothers failed time and time again to hold true the promises of sobriety. They battled the courts and fought systems and worked through their laundry lists to remain a part of their child's life. And even if they couldn't win, they would spend years trying. But the harder the drug, the stronger its hold on the user.

I walked up to the nurses' station to get a report on meth-mom. She wants to give the baby up for adoption. My heart dropped, but courage unwavering. I looked over to the bundled baby boy nestled in the clear rolling crib. He was sound asleep, unknowing. How could anyone, especially his own mother, not want him?

Giving birth is exhausting emotionally and physically and the circumstances can be overwhelming, but surely if she knew she were supported... would she really?... how could she want to? Some addicted moms have tried the battle before and know they can't win because they can't quit using. Other children who are lost to the state child welfare system leave evidence of their struggle. She wasn't them.

I used to believe that my personal self and my professional self were two different sides. I learned, though, that my boundaries are different in these two settings, but my Christian morals need to be able to thrive in each.

I sat down at the table and thought about my approach with this mother. My first thought was relief, as she could have gotten an abortion but, instead, chose life for her child. Then I cringed at the thought of a mother choosing to hand over that life. It's not my place, personally or professionally, to judge this mother. So, what was my place? As a social worker and as a Christian, I knew immediately I needed to *love* her. I prayed for the words and I prayed for the use of silence.

I didn't take my pad of paper or pen with me. As she lay in bed, I sat on the chair next to her. I leaned on my knees and looked her in the eyes. We talked. She asked questions and so did I. She poured out her struggles and I listened. I provided information and she pondered. I used the silence in the room and she wept.

I supported her and loved her as best I could. She didn't want him to be alone. She wanted him to know how special he was. She didn't want him to hate her. She didn't want to screw up her two daughters at home any more than she felt she already had done. She believed she had no business raising another child. She would go home and wish the whole thing had never happened. At her request, I called the adoption agency and they started the paperwork an hour later.

I walked out of the room unfeeling. I hadn't failed, as it wasn't my intent to win her over. Yet, I felt I hadn't succeeded either, as she was giving him up. She didn't even want to try. She just quit. Chin up, I kept with the plan to love her. I didn't understand this needless anguish, but I loved her.

Sitting at the nurses' station, I started to take notes on the highlights of our conversation. A veteran nurse had bundled the baby boy and was now feeding him and burping him. She bounced him and asked what his name was. I told her he didn't have one yet. So, she started rattling off names and asked the other nurses if he looked more like a Kyler or a Gramm. She said he would be at the hospital another day or two to observe for signs of detox. Then she was sure family preservation services would be working with his mom. I interjected that his biological mother would be putting him up for adoption. The nurse picked him up so he was facing her. She smiled so big and said, "You are going to make your new family so happy."

I checked in with his mother later in the afternoon so she could sign releases of information for the adoption agency. There was a peace settling into her face and shoulders. She told me the agency was to provide her a book of family profiles to go through. They invited her daughters to help pick out the baby's new adoptive family. She could go home tonight and sleep in her own bed knowing he would be cared for. This was certainly true as every nurse on shift tonight was a surrogate mother sharing in his care and nurturing him.

The day's events weighed on me as I sat to report on its happenings. He was a beautiful bundled baby boy. He was unique and wonderful and special... and unwanted. Tears came to the corners of my eyes. I looked around my office at pictures of my two baby boys. I couldn't imagine... I can't even fathom not wanting them. My world would be turned upside down if I knew that's what needed to happen for me to retain my responsibility and honor of being allowed by God to be their mother. How could she?

I closed my eyes and prayed. Lord we need you. How very lowly she must feel about herself to forfeit the mothering of her child. I prayed she would know how special and capable she was in the eyes of the Lord. I prayed that she would know God was going to use her gift for wonderful things. I prayed the bundled baby boy would never feel unwanted. I prayed he would know every minute of every day he was loved. I prayed for peace and comfort for everyone touched by this event.

My own sons stayed at their father's house tonight, as I had to work late. I almost started to be irritated that the mothers' lack of caring for their own children was taking away the time I got to spend with mine. I quickly let those feelings of resentment fade. I hadn't given all day to God to be overcome now. My mobile rang, and I wished my sons a goodnight. I told them how much I loved them at least five times. They were encouraged to say their prayers and to have sweet dreams. They would be mine again tomorrow.

One of the nurses came to finish her shift charting at the empty computer desk outside my office. She popped in the door and we shared the shocks and awes of our day. She turned on music from her phone as we both typed away. The tune, first muffled, now became clear, and all my worries washed away. We listened to Christian rock radio for the last hour of work. God is good.

It was very nice having God a part of my workday. I should pray more for the patients I work with. I'm definitely going to invite God to be in all areas of my life as I've done today, including in my professional one. Maybe the sun will come out tomorrow.

CHAPTER 6: IT'S A BOY

Chapter 7:
The Mad Woman

I t really was turning out to be a fantastic day. I was flying high with the Holy Spirit. Meth mom returned with an adoptive family already picked out. By the end of the day, the bundled baby boy would have a new family. It had to have been the best day ever for that couple. Can you imagine getting that call? Wow.

I took a late lunch and decide to scroll through Facebook. A younger gal I am Facebook friends with posted a surprising message with a picture of a church sign attached. The sign was very familiar. It was my mother's church… Hmmmm.

The young woman went to the same high school as I did, but just a few grades below me. It amazes me sometimes how very different people end up though their upbringing seems so similar in so many ways. Many of the people who influenced her while growing up were probably the same folks who influenced me.

Sign at the Methodist Church Main Entrance read: "THE ABSURD LIFE WITHOUT GOD: NO VALUE."

Her post read, "Love seeing a message that my life has no value. Shocker-this does not leave me with the urgency to run inside."

Initially, the comments featured a parade of people, some of whom I knew, making idle comments such as "Methodists are usually so chill," "Hahaha same, I value your life," and "an incredibly unwelcoming message." Two ladies from the church responded that it was the title of "a great sermon series." The young lady's sister replied, "A great sermon series on how to be self-righteous." Whoa, whoa, whoa! Now, that's not okay. Then someone, I will refer to simply as the "mad woman" added to her comment, "The hypocrisy is incredible, right? Like, if you are Christian you can sit on a pedestal and look down upon those who have different thoughts. But if you were raised religious, expanded your mind, studied religious histories in college, gone to various types of churches, still didn't 'get it' and left organized religion because SIMPLY LOVING without proclaiming a god was good enough for you – well in that case, you hold no value. You should have continued being complacent instead of evolving to better align with your own truth. STOP IT CHRISTIANS. You are not better than anyone, and by harassing people with differing beliefs, you are making a mockery of the faith you are in defense of." WOW. Now it was clear the mad woman had a deeper issue going on than just this church sign. But her comment was appalling and outright attacking Christians. Not just one person, one church, or one church sign, but the entire faith.

This was not okay with me. It was settling like oil in water and I was ready to set it on fire. I could identify with some of what she said. My mother took me to church every Sunday, so I too was raised religious. I had also expanded my mind through education and different church and religious experiences. I even can say that simply loving folks was a good thing. But then, she lost me with the ridiculous rhetoric on how she believes Christians are harassing and make a mockery of the faith. I wasn't about to tolerate this bullying behavior from the mad woman (MW), but I don't typically engage or even entertain this stuff and especially not on social media. Did I have a dog in this fight?... Absolutely.

Me: You may have missed the message here... how easy it must be to view Christians as on a pedestal from you soap box, I hardly find a sign on church property to be harassing... being a Christian is not saying mine is better than yours it's more like one beggar showing another beggar where the bread is... how "simply loving" is it for you to judge?

MW: Oh hello! Please help me understand what "the absurd life without god: no value" means. It clearly is presenting a "this group vs. that group" mentality.

Me: The above comments say it's a sermon series and probably has meaning for folks going to the church and listening to that sermon series... I hardly believe they put it up to create an us vs. them agenda... to outsiders I agree it could be misconstrued, as it obviously has a kind of scared straight message that really may not work for some folks

MW: That is fair, and I, of course, could not speak to the content in the sermon itself. What I am doing is reacting to the objective reality of what the sign says. It is isolating non-believers and suggesting their life has less worth than believers. That is not love. Whatever the purpose for the sign, it was not effective in welcoming or promoting openness.

Random citizen: I don't get this billboard... you'd think this church would want to be welcoming to other people (smh)... obviously not!! You are valuable, your view matters... they do not get that at all. You're right, many Christian churches think this same way... I'm glad you posted this; it makes me angry (insert red-faced angry emoticon)

This was beginning to infuriate me (Insert emoticon face with smoke coming out its ears). Lord help me keep my cool and respond with your words, not my emotions. Jesus told his disciples in Luke 12:11-12 "When you are brought before synagogues, rulers, and authorities, do not worry about how you will defend yourselves or what you will say, for the Holy Spirit will teach you at that time what you should say." I prayed he would give me the words I needed to show honor and glory to his name in the face of opposition.

MW: Also, one beggar showing another beggar where the bread is love because bread gives life. Religion does not.

Me: Exactly bread is love and it does sustain… religion is not the point of Christianity, it's Christ! He is the way the truth and the life (insert smiley face) Church is meant to be a safe pantry for bread giving and for beggars to support each other… religion is a hard label; it's more about relationships

MW: Just pointing out that millions and millions of people are alive without Christ. He may be YOUR way and truth and life… but a starving person cannot be kept alive because they believe in your guy in the sky. That is not a fact. Your beliefs should absolutely be respected, but beliefs are not facts.

Me: Life on earth is not the life-giving Christ is representing… a starving person can't live but he can be saved (insert smiley face)… he is not a guy in the sky, not at all. In fact, I look down to talk to him not up… my beliefs are based on the Bible, which is full of facts

MW: Ok, again. Like- I totally get what you are saying. I spent most of my life as a Christian, do you remember me sharing that? No, the Bible is FAR from factual. No, you have zero proof that a starving man who dies will be anything but an expired body soon to rot in the ground. You can BELIEVE what you wish, again- I am trying to make that known. I am not attacking your beliefs, but do not call them facts. Facts require proof, solid proof. Evidence supportive proof. So please, just go on your way believing what you will within the privacy of your own life.

Random Citizen: I'm a Christian and I find the sign really offensive. I don't think your personal view is on the chopping block here. But you are responding in a very defensive way. And as a Christian, I think Christians can be pretty judgy. The issue is more about how offensive is the sign.

I chose not to even touch her assault on the Bible. I was starting to pity her. Yes, I remembered how she said she grew up religious. My heart broke for her soul. 2 Peter 2:20-21 "If they have escaped the corruption of the world by knowing our Lord and Savior Jesus Christ and are again entangled in it and are overcome, they are worse off at the end that they were at the beginning. It would have been better for them not to have known the way of righteousness, than to have known it and then to turn their backs on the sacred command that was passed on to them." I needed to get back to work. There appeared to be no end to this debate.

Me: Lunch break is over but let me just say… it is not right to base an entire religion on a single verse just like it is not fair to judge that religion on one sign… you can openly defy that church and their sign along with an entire faith in a public setting, but don't you dare say I should stay private in defending and believing the same faith you openly ridicule. That, my friend, is hypocrisy

MW: Yup. I agree that is not right to base an entire religion on a single verse on a sign. Many people I love are religious, and many Christian. I understand their relationship with faith, and I imagine it's similar to yours. The call to respect both people who are different, and the call to respect facts vs. beliefs are the only issues I hoped to speak too. It's unfortunate your defensiveness about your personal life and faith has hindered you from seeing what I pointed out being hypocritical. You can't pick and choose what to defend and what to ignore. That does not help us have a respectful conversation. But it's cool; do your thing. *Young woman-* I still feel for you. Thanks for being truthful to yourself, which I'm sure makes you the point of ridicule more times than not.

Sigh Matthew 10:22 "You will be hated by everyone because of me, but the one who stands firm to the end will be saved." I did not respond, though I very much wanted the last word. That was my emotion talking though. I stood firm. The phone was turned off and I, indeed, ended my lunch break and returned to work.

Hours later after the work day was over... I returned to Facebook to see if there were any new developments. There were many likes for the young woman and the mad woman's comments. The young woman was apparently friends with many like-minded people, as most of us are. The audience was deaf to my defense.

YW: *ME*, the whole point was that the sign makes it seem that the only way one can have a life with value is through "god." I don't think anyone was stating you don't have the right to believe what you want or attacking you for those beliefs. It was honestly sickening to me to read the board. And it only further perpetuated the feelings of isolation we often feel living here.

MW: ^this right here

Me: Why would a church sign meant for members of that church sicken you? Are you a nonbeliever? Do you not belong to that church? Ok fine the sign wasn't meant for you then... I didn't take this as a personal attack anymore than you did... I have a problem with people saying it's ok to use your right to freedom of speech except Christians that we should have freedom of speech except Christians that it's ok to use your right to freedom of speech even if it offends others except Christians.

YW: I think you are still misunderstanding the point. I'm not saying the sign should be taken down or advocating that the in slightest. I am not for censoring. I was shocked by the message of "without god; no value." The hatefulness of the message surprised/shocked me. I am still very much in support of freedom of speech, even when it's hateful.

Me: This is hate speech now? Wow *YW* that is overreaching... there is clearly a disconnect between that sign's intention and your interpretation... I promise that God and Jesus Christ including every person that goes to that church would never say that a nonbeliever has no value... Christianity is based in love. Jesus loves you; he values your life.

MW: So explain who put this sign up then. Are you suggesting a non-church-goer did it? Are you unable to read what the sign clearly says? The "disconnect" lies between one of these very simple and obvious items.

Me: That might be a good question I would encourage you to attend church on Sunday and find out for yourself... spend some time with the pastor asked him what the sign means and why it was put up in such a way

MW: *Me*, Why would I? According to this sign my life has 'no value.' Why is it MY job to come FIND OUT what the INTENTION was behind the sign? Oh yea- it's not my job.

Me: *MW*, The members of the church that have responded say it is a sign with wording based on a sermon about Solomon's discovery of wisdom I wasn't there but would love to hear more... but I'm certainly not going to overreach and look at that statement to say that people don't have value… It's not your job to find out I was only encouraging you to gain a better understanding

MW: *Me,* I don't have a problem with the sermon, nor do I think anyone in this thread does. The problem is, that this sign does not connect any dots. The members who are familiar with the link between this sign and the sermon, they get it. But the outside world (aka *YW* on her drive) would have NO idea what the sign means. It should not be her job to explore it and understand why it comes off so offensively. Instead, this church should use better judgment so that they don't use thoughtless arrangements of words that result this way. If signs use words that are thoughtless and result in offending and frustrating non-members, that is not a positive result. Why would it benefit a church to essentially suggest that non-believers do not have a life with value? It wouldn't. So they shouldn't have posted this.

Me: It wasn't a thoughtless sign actually it sounds like a very purposeful sign created for people who attend that church. It was not a message to the masses to gain your membership… unbelievers will not understand; people who don't go to that church will not understand… I have a problem with people who want to publicly ridicule a church sign with no effort for understanding. So, you know what? You will find what you are looking for. If you're looking for the good, you will find good. If you were looking for the bad and offensive, you too will find it

Well, I certainly didn't get the last word in as commentary poured in from the young woman's friends and family who were following the comments and chose to weigh in on the topic. A few were from church members and one even posted 28 bible verses about living without God. There were 86 comments in all. The sign remained until the sermon series ended.

I realized there were many who came to this young woman's defense, yet I felt abandoned. If I made such a point on my Facebook page, would my Facebook friends be of similar mind? It started to make me think. I didn't have one person on Facebook from my church family. Why not? I thought about what I post and maybe concerned at times I can be too liberal or too vulgar for their taste. Looking inward, this is my problem, not theirs. I should be more mindful of what I post. I should set more of an example as a Christian and ensure I am spreading the right messages.

As I discovered through my birthday encouragement countdown, essentially hitting that "like" button is telling the system "send me more like that!" I searched and started adding those from my church family as friends on Facebook. Their presence is powerful. If you have to wonder "what would my church think about this post?", then what more would Jesus have to say about it. Would He follow me? Would He be my friend? Would He smile or laugh out loud at the jokes I shared? If "my story" were read, would it point to God, or would you even know I was a Christian?

CHAPTER 7: THE MAD WOMAN

CHAPTER 8:
SOME RELIEF

Financial Peace University has come to an end. I have so much enjoyed this journey. It's the first Wednesday without this group and I miss them. The honest, nonjudgmental support was so encouraging. I don't feel like a gazelle, as this process of saving money is a slow one for me with only $180 in savings. I do feel the intensity though and more disciplined now than ever with my finances. I have a budget and have made some solid decisions lately.

It is hard to stay committed. I have upcoming medical needs for my kids that will be quite expensive. Credit card usage is very tempting, but I will not be moved. I am planning and saving now and pray it will be enough. God provides.

Interestingly too, God uses us as a blessing to others. Remember me saying I had two mortgages? Well, my old house was being rented out. I received notification the tenant would be moving out. What was I going to do? I can't afford two mortgages and finding a renter is burdensome. The property management company I had worked with the last year was awful. I didn't want to continue getting charged hidden fees.

I was lying in bed early one morning when I scrolled Facebook to find a post by an old coworker of mine. She is an adult educator and teaches a GED glass at the local vocational college. She described how she had taken on a new student. He was homeless and working on his education. He needed a place to live while he continued to work and go to school.

I reached out to her. It was a complete "God thing." My rental home would be occupied saving me from two mortgage payments or even foreclosure. This young man would also get a home, something he may not have had in a very long time. It was a win-win deal.

~ ~ ~

I have been broken this week. Blow after blow, my world was shaken and as I looked around the walls around me fell. I was left bruised and vulnerable and in the darkest of places. But God is good. We know this, even when we can't see it. My family is suffering from illnesses unseen, and my job, my livelihood, is being threatened. Like a fool, I fell down. I grabbed bottle after bottle and blew through a pack of cigarettes. These chains I had broken a year ago quickly took hold in my weakest moment.

When I got off work today, my plan was simple. I grabbed a pack of cigarettes and bottle of wine. Sickened and lonely, I was ashamed how easily I had turned away from God. In the midst of sorrow and self-loathing, hope came through the clouds shining its light and love on my face like the warmth of sun. Sun and rain at the same time, how completely lovely it was.

I did something that surprised me; I went to the bookshelf and grabbed my leather-bound Bible. I have had this Bible for years. I should be ashamed at how clean the cover is and how unworn the pages are. Turning randomly to Philippians, I started reading. Paul was lonely you can hear it in his voice. The world was awful, and he yearned to be with Christ again. He knew he needed to stay though. He knew he needed to stay for us. We needed him to continue spreading the gospel. His stand gave us all permission to stand with him. Our fears are nothing when what you're doing is for good.

Inspired. I have a few ideas on how to move forward. God willing one of them might materialize. Knowing if I do it for good, God is with me and there's no fear. I said it before and I'll say it again. I should pray more. God and I need to talk this through. I need to have more conversations with him like I did tonight. He answers; he really does. In the songs I hear on the radio, through the people He has put in my life, and with the nudges He gives to pick up my Bible and read, He speaks to me. I pray Lord for wisdom and for a listening ear to your words.

I absolutely love this view of prayer I got in a letter from a friend:

"You say you prayed for patience and peace. Do you find peace in prayer? Does it soothe you when you speak to God? I find it does. To a point anyway to unburden worries and pain to someone? God especially. But it's like a pill, a temporary lift. Should we pop one prayer in the morning? One before bed? If anything aches or bothers you throughout the day, a dose here or there may help? Ibuprofen limits its doses. Hard on the liver they say. I bet you could pop prayer all day with no liver problems! Just sayin'."

I love this perspective so much. New goal is to pop that prayer all day long!

Chapter 8: Some Relief

CHAPTER 9:
THE LOST LETTER

Jesus being killed. Crucified. How is that "dying for our sins"? What's the relation? I don't understand it. And it's the common phrase. The Lord gave his son so that we may be forgiven? What does His death have to do with me being forgiven? If Jesus hadn't died on the cross, would God not forgive anyone? Can you explain this to me? Cause I don't get it.

My friend asked the most amazing question. It led me to examine my beliefs and test my knowledge. I grew up going to church, thanks to my mother. Every Sunday was Sunday school then worship and a sermon. There were vacation Bible schools, summer camps, and youth conferences. I heard it over and over and grew up taking for granted it was common knowledge. So much so that I was shocked when these questions were asked of me... What does his death have to do with forgiveness? Uhm everything! Man, oh man, do I take that knowledge for granted.

Here is what I came up with in response to this important series of questions:

The Bible has two sections: the Old Testament and the New Testament. In order to understand the New Testament, you need to have an appreciation of the old one.

Genesis 3:22 "And the Lord God said, "The man has now become like one of us, knowing good and evil. He must not be allowed to reach out his hand and take also from the tree of life and eat and live forever." We were sinful and were not then allowed to live forever on earth. No doubt, Adam and Eve lived for a long time (Genesis 5:5, Adam was 930 when he died) and sired many sons and daughters to populate the Earth. But ultimately, they died and so will we.

Genesis 6:5-8 Summarized… The Lord saw how great the wickedness of the human race had become on the earth… regretted that he had made human beings… decided to wipe from the face of the earth the human race and all creatures that move along the ground. But Noah found favor in the eyes of the Lord. Because… Noah was righteous and walked faithfully with God (Genesis 6:9).

Noah was 500 years old when he became a father of Shem, Ham, and Japheth (Genesis 5:32). And you thought your old man was old! He builds the ark with his sons exactly as God instructed. The flood waters came when Noah was 600 years old (Genesis 7:6).

FUN FACT- It is commonly known that the animals went on to the ark two by two. However, in Genesis 7:1-3, you read that there was one pair of every kind of *unclean* animal. But there were SEVEN pairs of every kind of clean animal and SEVEN pairs of every kind of bird. My Sunday school lessons didn't mention this little tidbit.

It rained for 40 days and 40 nights (Genesis 7:12). The waters flooded the earth for 150 days (Genesis 7:24). It took longer still, Noah was 601 and one month (Genesis 8:13) but finally the earth was completely dry. Noah came out of the ark with his family along with all the creatures. Noah built an altar to the Lord and, taking some of all the clean animals and clean birds, he sacrificed burnt offerings on it (Genesis 8:20). See? It was a good thing there were seven pairs, or those creatures would have survived a flood only to have been sacrificed.

Genesis 8:21-22 summarized… The Lord smelled the pleasing aroma and said in his heart he would never again curse the ground or destroy all living creatures because of humans even though he knows the human heart is evil from childhood.

Genesis 9 summarized… God establishes a covenant with Noah and with his descendants after him and with every living creature that came out of the ark. He promised never again will all life be destroyed by the waters of a flood; never again will there be a flood to destroy the earth (Genesis 9:11). God set a rainbow in the clouds as a sign of the covenant between him and the earth (Genesis 9:14-15).

So, Noah's family multiplied the earth. One of Shem's descendants many years and generations later included a righteous Hebrew man named Abraham (Genesis 11:26). Abraham married Sarah (Genesis 11:29). Genesis 12 summarized… Lord called Abraham and promised to bless him and make him into a great nation. All the people on Earth were to be blessed through Abraham. Genesis 13/14 summarized… Abraham becomes very wealthy. Wherever he went, he built an altar to the Lord. (We know from Noah this sacrifice of clean animals on an altar is pleasing to the Lord.) Any enemy of Abraham was defeated.

From Genesis 15- The Lord promised Abraham numerous offspring and possession of land which will become a great nation and he would be their God. God made a covenant with Abraham and every young male and newborns at 8 days old should be circumcised as a sign of the covenant (Genesis 17:10-12). Abraham did have many sons and many sons had father Abraham as the song goes. Ha-ha, you other Sunday school goers sang that last line, didn't you? Well Abraham's offspring were not all Sarah's kids. If you want a good Old Testament soap opera read the rest of Genesis which is full of shenanigans.

History goes on and eventually leads us to Moses. By then, the Hebrews had become slaves to the Egyptian pharaoh who was worried they were too numerous and would rise up against him (Exodus 1). God speaks to Moses and sends him to Pharaoh to bring his people out of Egypt (Exodus 3). God speaks to Moses about the covenant he had with Abraham and reminded them he was their God and would deliver them (Exodus 6). The plagues on Egypt were God's signs and wonders as mighty acts to bring his people out of Egypt to the wilderness to worship him (Exodus 7). The plagues brought fear to Pharaoh and he let God's people go. They crossed the Red Sea to the wilderness at Mount Sinai.

God has Moses and his brother, Aaron, meet him up on Mount Sinai. There he gives them ten laws known as The Ten Commandments. He tells them to make an altar and sacrifice on it burnt offerings and fellowship offerings (Exodus 20:1-23).

The covenant is confirmed in Exodus 24. God gives Moses tablets of stone with the law and commandments written on them (Exodus 24:12). The rest of Exodus is filled with numerous instructions from the Lord regarding offerings etc. All laws were super specific and requiring the people of God atonement for their lives (Exodus 30:16). When God was done giving instruction to Moses on Mount Sinai, he provided Moses two tablets of the covenant on stone literally inscribed by the finger of God (Exodus 31:18).

FUN FACT: While Moses stayed up on the mountain with God for 40 days and 40 nights (Exodus 24:18), the people who were just freed from slavery by God quickly turned sour. They took all their gold and melted it into the shape of a calf. They worshipped and made offerings to it. When Moses came down from the mountain and saw this despicable scene, he was furious. In fact, he was so mad he *threw* the tablets inscribed by God and they broke! (Exodus 32:19). Talk about awkward and embarrassing! God had to make Moses another set of stone tablets like the first ones (Exodus 34:4). WHOOPS!

Lots of rules and regulations followed and the people of God made offerings and sacrifices as atonement for their lives. The aroma continued to be pleasing to God. They also made sin offerings when they broke any of Lord's commands (Leviticus 4:2). They made guilt offerings when unfaithful to the Lord (Leviticus 5:15). Both came with specific laws and regulations to follow. The people of God lived under "the law" for a long time.

Jeremiah 31:31-34: "The days are coming," declares the Lord, "when I will make a new covenant with the people of Israel and with the people of Judah. It will not be like the covenant I made with their ancestors when I took them by the hand to lead them out of Egypt, because they broke my covenant, though I was a husband to them," declares the Lord. "This is the covenant I will make with the people of Israel after that time," declares the Lord. "I will put my law in their minds and write it on their hearts. I will be their God, and they will be my people. No longer will they teach their neighbor, or say to one another, 'Know the Lord,' because they will all know me, from the least of them to the greatest," declares the Lord. "For I will forgive their wickedness and will remember their sins no more." This is also said in Hebrews 8:8-12. Hebrews 8:13 further says, "By calling this covenant "new", he has made the first one obsolete; and what is obsolete and outdated will soon disappear."

Wow. We were all made to be God's people. He has a plan. No longer will we be required atonement for sin. God will forgive and forget our sins. This is incredible and a foreshadowing, if you will, of the amazing events to come. God tells us a new covenant is coming.

Matthew 1:1-17 Complete genealogy is listed showing Jesus as a descendant of Abraham with whom God made the old covenant. His name is Jesus because "he will save his people from their sins" (Matthew 1:21).

"We are God's offspring, we should not think that the divine being is like gold or silver or stone- an image made by human design and skill [not an idol]. In the past, God overlooked such ignorance [like that nonsense on Mount Sinai with the gold calf], but now he commands all people everywhere to repent [ask forgiveness]. For he has set a day when he will judge the world with justice by the man he has appointed [Jesus]. He has given proof of this to everyone by raising him from the dead" (Acts 17:29-31). Very cool.

So, I told you all that so you could better understand and appreciate this…

Hebrews 9:11-28 "But when Christ came as high priest of the good things that are now already here, he went through the greater and more perfect tabernacle that is not made with human hands, that is to say, is not a part of this creation. He did not enter by means of the blood of goats and calves; but he entered the Most Holy Place once for all by his own blood, thus obtaining eternal redemption. The blood of goats and bulls and the ashes of a heifer sprinkled on those who are ceremonially unclean sanctify them so that they are outwardly clean. How much more, then, will the blood of Christ, who through the eternal Spirit offered himself unblemished to God, cleanse our consciences from acts that lead to death, so that we may serve the living God!"

Stay with me!...

"For this reason Christ is the mediator of a new covenant, that those who are called may receive the promised eternal inheritance—now that he has died as a ransom to set them free from the sins committed under the first covenant. In the case of a will, it is necessary to prove the death of the one who made it, because a will is in force only when somebody has died; it never takes effect while the one who made it is living. This is why even the first covenant was not put into effect without blood. When Moses had proclaimed every command of the law to all the people, he took the blood of calves, together with water, scarlet wool and branches of hyssop, and sprinkled the scroll and all the people. He said, "This is the blood of the covenant, which God has commanded you to keep." In the same way, he sprinkled with blood both the tabernacle and everything used in its ceremonies. In fact, the law requires that nearly everything be cleansed with blood, and without the shedding of blood, there is no forgiveness. It was necessary, then, for the copies of the heavenly things to be purified with these sacrifices, but the heavenly things themselves with better sacrifices than these. For Christ did not enter a sanctuary made with human hands that was only a copy of the true one; he entered heaven itself, now to appear for us in God's presence. Nor did he enter heaven to offer himself again and again, the way the high priest enters the Most Holy Place every year with blood that is not his own. Otherwise Christ would have had to suffer many times since the creation of the world. But he has appeared once for all at the culmination of the ages to do away with sin by the sacrifice of himself. Just as people are destined to die once, and after that to face judgment, so Christ was sacrificed once to take away the sins of many; and he will appear a second time, not to bear sin, but to bring salvation to those who are waiting for him."

THAT is why Jesus had to die and THAT is why he is the Savior of the World. "A new covenant- not of the letter [the law] but of the Spirit [belief]; for the letter kills, but the Spirit gives life" (2 Corinthians 3:6). "For God so loved the world that he gave his one and only Son, that whoever believes in him shall not perish but have eternal life. For God did not send his Son into the world to condemn the world, but to save the world through him" (John 3:16-17). Put that on a poster!

Garth Brooks' famous song Unanswered Prayers is recorded at 3 minutes and 14 seconds. John 3:14 mentions Moses who died before making it to the Promise Land. Coincidence? Ha-ha, I like to think not. I digress.

CHAPTER 10:
I'VE GOT FRIENDS IN LOW PLACES

I have been a fan of Garth Brooks since I was a kid. When I was a tween, my fandom quickly turned into a celebrity crush. I knew every song and had every CD. So, when my aunt asked me if I wanted to go to his concert, I about regressed into a teen-like state and screamed. I was soooo excited.

It had been a long time since I wore boots and jeans or anything resembling the country girl wardrobe of my younger-years. I did the best I could with what I had. A pink lace shirt with daisies, blue jeans, and brown boots. I met my aunt at the doorway and butterflies filled my stomach. I couldn't believe I was going to see Garth Brooks live!

We found our seats in the auditorium. Great seats too, my aunt did an awesome job! It was a sold-out show. One by one the stadium filled with excited fans. Garth Brooks! The man! The legend! After the pre-concert entertainment, Garth blasts onto the stage. The packed crowd went crazy, screaming, hooping and hollering, whistles, and "we love you Garth" echoed and filled every corner of the stadium. He was an entertainer and didn't disappoint.

Garth Brooks danced across the stage like a wild bull on fire! The crowd just loved it. He sang the old favorites and the new hits. Like a rehearsed choir, the fans sang along knowing every word of the lyrics. The energy was contagious.

I don't remember what song it was, but I know it was one of the slower ballads. Like fireflies lighting up the night sky, cellphone lights flickered on across the crowd. The illumination was glorious. My mind wandered off, odd as that was, considering the event around me. This was just Garth Brooks, a man. A simple man favored for his voice, lyrics, and ability to entertain. Can you imagine if it was Jesus on that stage? Can you imagine if it were angels singing around you instead of off-pitch Midwesterners? The thought and idea took hold of my heart, and I was overwhelmed. Tears came to my eyes, and my face glowed as a smile furnaced by a new fire in my soul overcame me.

This thought triggered a whole new series of questions in my head. How much would I pay for a stadium seat at a Jesus concert? How long would I stand in line? How much money would I pay for His t-shirt? If Garth Brooks sent shivers down my spine, how greater a feel of anticipation would I have waiting for an opportunity to stand in the presence of Jesus?... WOW, that will make you think.

CHAPTER 11:
BREAKING BAD NEWS WITH PUPPIES

My mother is the strongest woman of faith I've ever known. She's not only faithful but also believes with all her heart that the God she loves dearly, will save her. That love is unwavering and inspiring. God is bigger and more powerful than cancer. Being a Christian, a follower of Christ, doesn't make you immune to tragedy anymore than it makes you immune to cancer.

I was in the doctor's office next to my mother when we got the bad news. There is no good way to deliver bad news. It could be handed over in a basket with an adorable puppy, but you'd still be like "that's terrible news." The doctor's words were practiced as you would expect from an experienced oncologist. I don't think it would have mattered the delivery as the words fell cold and hard. Her cancer was back. There are two spots on her liver about an inch. "The burden of disease is small." It didn't feel small. Matthew 11:30 popped in my head: "For my yoke is easy and my burden is light."

We were so blessed. After surgery, radiation, and chemotherapy she was still with us. Most folks don't get six months and we had two years. Two years to the date exactly. It was this day in 2015, one of the worst years of my life, when we found out she had cancer.

The new spots warranted a change in treatment. The chemotherapy road had ended. I cried, hoping the end of that road didn't also mean the end for my mother.

We left the office and went to sit in the busy lobby. In the smallest corner we could find, we sat as a family. I don't remember what we were waiting for, but God did. Tears down our faces, the woman sitting next to us leaned over. She said she didn't know what we were going through but asked if she could pray with us. My mother breathed a sigh of relief as our Lord gave a complete stranger the words to speak to our hearts. I wished I had gotten the puppy.

CHAPTER 12:
WOW, GOD!

I have been going to my church for a few years now. With two young sons, it was hard enough getting us to Sunday school and church that I never felt like I could put in good effort volunteering. However, my kiddos were old enough now to participate in Vacation Bible School and the opportunity to take on this ministry at my church had been planting seeds in my mind and heart for months. I stepped out in faith and took on the endeavor.

For months, I reviewed materials, lesson plans, booklets, schedules, forms, etc. In the evening and weekends when I could borrow an hour or two, I carefully outlined and planned for the week-long event. This was the biggest volunteer undertaking I've ever done, and I am so glad I did it.

The theme was Maker Fun Factory and it was all about how wonderful God made us. There were creative crafts for all ages, videos, and fun science experiments. As the event leader, I mulled over just how involved I wanted to be. There was an ongoing challenge written in to identify amazing things God has created using all five senses. There were key phrases the leader was to say that would then prompt the kids to say, "Wow, God!" I would have missed a huge opportunity had I written this off. It was an "extra," but it turned out so awesome.

Keep in mind this is a small-town church, so when nearly 80 kids showed up it was exciting. We introduced "God Sightings." What amazing things do you see, hear, taste, touch, and smell that God created? Their answers were darling from the sound of a piano to the taste of watermelon.

Additionally, it was emphasized when you see someone being kind to another person that was also a "God Sighting."

The theme of the first day was "God Made You" Wow, God! The phrase was in every lesson and activity for the day. By the second day, the prompting was rare. The second day's theme was "God is for you," and children responded, "Wow, God!" "God is always with you" for the third day, "Wow, God!" By the fourth day there was no prompting, and you could truly feel the Holy Spirit move throughout the church. "God will always love you," "Wow, God!" The joy in the children's voices became music to our ears. It was so powerful.

The last day, it came full circle. I try to pray often, but very rarely out loud. The minister made it a point to tell me after the first day that a prayer should be said at least at the beginning and end of the day. Trying not to be scripted, I found prayers in the curriculum for the opening and closing sessions. The last day was themed "God made you for a reason". At the closing prayer, I'd call my words as "winging it." However, winging it was more likely the Holy Spirit giving me words to speak. Luke 12:11-12 "Do not worry about… what you will say, for the Holy Spirit will teach you at that time what you should say." Without thinking, I closed the prayer with "God is always with you." All the children, without prompting, yelled, "Wow, God!" It was a one-of-a-kind God Sighting and I will never forget it.

This experience was definitely one that changed my heart. Luke 6:38 Jesus tells us, "Give, and it will be given to you." I like to believe the children got a little closer to God this week, and I know I sure did.

CHAPTER 13:
MAY THE WORK I'VE DONE SPEAK FOR ME

I had just gotten to work when I received the call. I hate these calls and have received too many. The pain and sorrow in the voice that bears the bad news sends panic through every nerve and your heart weighs heavy in your chest. Papa H, as we all called him, couldn't get out of bed this morning. The ambulance came to pick him up and he likely suffered a major stroke.

As a social worker at the hospital, I knew what to do and have walked it through dozens of times with patients and their families. Although you can empathize, nothing hurts more like having to watch it happen in your own life. I quickly got in my car and left for a hospital in another town. So quick was the news and so hasty my response, I got to the emergency room before Papa H had arrived.

He came in and was settled into the room. His brain was bleeding out and there was no chance of recovery. Papa H was over 90 years old. He had made his wishes known and had even told us facetiously yet honestly if he went down to call the hearse not the ambulance. He feared being an "invalid." It was a hard, but necessary series of events.

Family was notified, tears were shed, and Papa H was made "comfortable." It was truly the most honorable end I've ever experienced. It was as it should be. I've seen too many unfortunate lives leave this world in the most horrible ways. Sorrow comes always, but hearts break with the tragedy. Fatal car accidents, cancer, and cardiac arrest had taken our loved ones in their forties and fifties. Papa H was 91. Last weekend, he was dancing and playing cards. Yesterday he had harvested walnuts and mowed the yard. He woke up one day, had a stroke, and by the end of the day would be in Heaven with his Savior. I felt great peace about his passing. It was the way death should be in my mind.

On Papa H's casket was written *MAY THE WORK I'VE DONE SPEAK FOR ME.*

CHAPTER 14:
WHAT IF?

My Dad died on this date. He was only 48 years old. He didn't pass one day, and he wasn't taken in an instant. It was an awful, horrible, three-year death of pain and suffering.

I feel every moment of sadness. Time doesn't fly for this kind of stuff. The grief drags on every birthday, every anniversary, every holiday, and every gathering as reminders of who is missing from the pictures.

After all this time, the emotion is still raw and the grief consuming. Not until recently have I figured out why it has never gotten better for me. I don't mourn the loss of the father I had as a child. He was incredibly supportive and provided for every need. That I have accepted and can think of with fond memory.

No, it is so hard to deal even a decade later because I'm mourning the friend I never got to know. I'm sad because I feel that loss every day. I'm angry when I hear someone say "I HAVE to call my dad; it's Father's Day" or birthday or whatever. You GET to call!

I cope by moving forward. There's no going back or figuring out how it could have been better. A "what if" world is a sad and dangerous place to live. So, I have and we all have, in one way or another and some sooner than others, chosen a road of hope and acceptance.

From the song sang at my dad's funeral, "the promise was when everything fell, we'd be held." Bad things happen, and no one is immune to tragedy. But you can use it to move forward.

Time doesn't heal people, God heals people. Praying, my heart heals a little each day from the hurt of missing him.

PART TWO

"I am not more than a wisp of smoke to the world, but to God I am a flame of hope and promise in a darkened room." Joan Noeldechen

CHAPTER 14: WHAT IF?

Chapter 15:
Keeping It Together

I don't want to live. I don't want to be here anymore. This life has been so full of pain and heart wrenching catastrophe. I've been sad for so long that I don't remember what it's like not to be depressed. My whole adult life has been a series of death, stress, and tragedy. I'm tired. I'm just done.

Sunday, I slept through church and instead picked up the kids at noon. I honestly didn't want to get them at all. That's when I knew my depression was full force. I love my kids and they're one of the few sources of joy in my life. When I'm so sad that I want to stay in that dark place, any light, even my children, are too much to bear. It's not okay. I should always want to be with my children. I'm their mother.

Getting through the rest of the day with them was so hard. I tried to keep it together. It was with great conscious effort that I got out of bed, fed them lunch and dinner, and listened to my son read his assignment for school the next day. I just wanted to sleep, but I knew my little one needs constant supervision. I fought every minute to be present for them, to hold the tears in, and be mom-like.

I felt like a complete failure for not getting up and getting them to church. God, Pastor, Sunday school teachers, and their classmates were surely disappointed in their absence. God is first; He should always be first, and I failed not only for myself, but more importantly for the boys.

Awakened this morning feeling no different, I tried to stick to my routine. Coffee brewed while I did some stretches, push-ups, and sit-ups. Creamer filled coffee taken out to the porch and I sat in my red chair. It was too dark still. The season of summer early morning light was nearly gone. The sun was still below the trees and the birds and squirrels not yet out to scrounge and squabble over breakfast. It was just me and the crickets.

The first cup of coffee having been consumed, I went inside to take a shower hoping the cleanliness would help. Dressed by 7am, I woke up the boys to get them ready for their day. Book bag was ready, homework completed, and progress report signed off on. Their dad came and took the older off to first grade. The younger was going with me this morning.

We packed a snack and off we went. He was a good little helper as we dropped off the recycling, paid the city bill, and got a few things at the general store. This was, of course, rewarded with a new hot wheel toy. We drove to the eye doctor, and he got to pick out new glasses. At the market, he got another toy and I bought one for his brother too so he wouldn't feel left out. When I don't feel like I can be a source of happiness for them, I often will buy a new toy that I know will make them happy.

I lost my primary care doctor and had a new appointment at a new office with a new primary care doctor. The youngest was with me and was running out of patience with our morning errands. His diaper was full which doesn't help, so I left the lobby with him to get a fresh diaper from the car. I looked across the hall and there was my first ex-husband. Ugh, I really could have gone without seeing him. A wave of hurt and resentment rushed over me.

We finished the job of changing the diaper and quickly went to the lobby avoiding any glances across the hall. I was hoping for a new place of sanctuary to get help, but I don't see me going back there beyond today.

I don't want to show up wondering if he'll be there and have to look or not look and pretend to not care.

When I made it back to see the physician, I became completely overwhelmed. Through my tears, I attempted to convey all the sources of stress in my life, and how currently I am not managing them correctly. I do need to exercise, yes, thanks for bringing up one more thing I am failing to do. He did increase the dosage of my antidepressant, which hopefully helps. I am to follow up in a month.

Youngest was happy again as we drove through a fast food place for a kid's meal. I refused to eat my feelings as I too often do, so ordered nothing and continued to drink my tea. At home, we unloaded the few bags of items. I turned on a show for him to watch. He wanted to play.

I was upset and tearful again. I didn't want to play. I should. I should WANT to play with my kid. He wanted to be with his mom and share his time with me, but I couldn't feel anything past the dark hole I had fallen into. I survived until 2pm and took him over to his dad's house.

Back at the house, I took my anxiety pill, three Tylenol PM tablets, and my antidepressant capsule. My alarm was set for 4:30p. I turned down the AC, turned on my ceiling fan, shut the blinds, and cried myself to sleep.

When I woke up, nothing seemed better. I didn't want to live anymore. I thought about if the razor blade in the kitchen would be sharp enough. I thought about the sheet hanging from the ceiling fan in the side room and if it would hold. I thought about all the pills in the house.

The kids' dad agreed to keep them for the night and I told him I wasn't well. Please tell the kids I was sick. Texting my therapist, she said there was an opening at 6p after work tomorrow. If I can just make it until then,

I needed help. I wanted someone to come and make sure I was safe. I wanted someone to take the pills, sheets, and razors. I wanted to call for help. I need help. I don't WANT to think this way.

I stayed in my bed, frozen, afraid if I got up, I was going to act on these thoughts. I cried and fell back asleep.

Chapter 16:
Can't Keep It Together Any Longer

It was 3am when I woke up. I was done. I didn't want to live anymore. I walked into the kitchen and grabbed the razor blade. Pulling up the left sleeve of my shirt, I saw my "held" tattoo. The words of the song echoed in my head. The world is not falling apart, it's falling into place, you're not alone, let go, and just be held. I pressed the razor against my skin right below the word. I pressed and slid the razor about an inch. It wasn't sharp enough.

I saw the coffee mug my mother gave me with a scripture on the outside. Romans 8:28. I had made myself memorize the verse since it seemed to mean so much to her. "God works for the good of those who love him."

I needed a plan, so I packed my bag with clothes for three days. I will try to get ready for work, I will try to get through the day, and I will go see my therapist at 6p. If I can't make it, I will take my bag to the psychiatric hospital and check myself in. I will call my insurance company when I get to work so I know which hospital would be in network. I tried to cut with the razor again, but it still isn't going through my skin deep enough.

It is time to wait it out. I prayed for a still mind, a courageous heart, and a body that wouldn't betray me. My kids need their mother, a good one.

…

I am writing now from behind locked doors. I couldn't make it through the day, so now at a psychiatric hospital. This place is a strange mix between prison and a hotel. Dayrooms, locked doors, limited property, yet you get to watch television, eat snacks, and smoke cigarettes. I was glad to have packed a bag, but unfortunately forgot shoes. Good thing I can rock out these grey gripper socks.

My blood pressure was really high, 168/118. The stress has really gotten to me. I'm not used to being around so many people and not used to just sitting around. There are no cell phones allowed for patients, so not sure what to do with myself.

Today, my brother was there for me. He was nice enough to leave work to pick me up and bring me here. He was supportive and not upset like I thought he might be. I texted my mom on the way and hope she's not upset.

Everything about life has got me down right now: work, kids, family, kids' school, and people being hateful and dumb. People are dying, and others are being incredibly selfish. This is the sad saga of my life.

They asked me an interesting question during the admission assessment. After checking the box stating I was a Christian, the assessor asked, "What does your religion say about suicide?" It was my understanding that if you committed suicide, you would go to hell. I don't remember reading that anywhere in the Bible, though. However, I do know that God is life and is in control of who lives and who dies. It would be wrong for someone to take that control into their own hands.

CHAPTER 17:
WORRY PURGE

I'm sure my friends are cussing me by now because I haven't answered my phone. I can't use my phone at all. This has been really frustrating. They say it's because of HIPAA, but that's likely a lie, since every staff member seems to be on their phones constantly.

Group therapies today were interesting and some of the topics hit home. There are a few loudmouths dominating the group and one lady especially complains about every little thing. Everyone else seems to carry their pain around just like me. They are up and down and cry at the drop of a hat, like me. It's a good bunch overall, very chill and nonjudgmental.

In one group session, we were challenged to do a "worry purge." Given a few minutes, we wrote down everything we were worrying about. I filled the page easily from my mother dying, cheating men, my kids, the happiness of my family, careers, pain, loneliness, health, loss of loved ones, finances, not feeling connected with other believers, etc. How easy it was to assume all this responsibility as if I had direct influence and control over everything!

Matthew 6:25 "Do not worry about your life, what you will eat or drink; or about your body... Can any one of you by worrying add a single hour to your life?" Matthew 6:34 "Do not worry about tomorrow, for tomorrow will worry about itself. Each day has enough trouble of its own."

The next activity in group was to outline first "right now I am" then reframe it to "I want to be".

Right now, I am _____	I want to be _____
Down	Happy
Unsatisfied	Content
Anxious	At peace
Tired	Energetic
Messy	Healthy
Down-trodden	Hopeful
Failing	Successful
Emotional	Manageable
Stuck	Moving forward
Impulsive	Steadfast
Trying	Working
Cautious	Confident

I want to be so different than I am now. It's unsettling. How did I get so off track?

I saw my therapist today and she was very good at helping me redirect and focus on myself rather than absorbing the feelings and problems of others. She provided some validation for me as a mother and helping professional. It tore me apart to know I was going to have to be here through the weekend. But she said she would be worried about me if I left.

I don't feel relevant in my own life right now. She said something very powerful, "you matter." I may have to accept this is more than a three-day stay.

James 4:7-10 "Submit yourselves, then, to God. Resist the devil, and he will flee from you. Come near to God and he will come near to you. Wash your hands, you sinners, and purify your hearts, you double-minded. Grieve, mourn and wail. Change your laughter to mourning and your joy to gloom. Humble yourselves before the Lord, and he will lift you up."

My psychiatrist's visit was helpful too. She listened intently as I told her my story and the events leading up to my admission here. She was kind enough to increase my dose of antidepressants and started me on a mood stabilizer. I very much hope it helps. My emotions have been all over the place, and, hour by hour, it could be different. It's exhausting, and I'm so tired.

I asked for help. I attended groups and completed the assignments. I'm eating well and even exercising. I talked and socialized. I'm being honest with myself and others. I'm trying. I'm trying so very hard. I don't feel like doing any of it, but I have to, as it's the only way to get better. The Lord's strength moves me, not my own.

"Don't stop when you're tired. Stop when you're done." —David Goggins

CHAPTER 17: WORRY PURGE

CHAPTER 18:
GOING THROUGH THE MOTIONS

It looks like I'll be here through the weekend. Therapist told me not to rush; it's a process. This is still very frustrating. There was seriously a class today on breathing. Apparently, there's a wrong way to do it. Who knew? I'm going to groups and taking my medications, so hoping it gets better over time. I do feel less anxious today, so that's something.

A group today discussed the idea of radical acceptance. It separates out what you can control versus what you can't control. What you can't control you acknowledge as such. You don't have to like it or agree with it. It is what it is. Letting go is hard. Even letting go of a false sense of control is painful.

I miss my kids something fierce. I came to a hospital out of town, so I wouldn't have a chance of knowing anyone. However, it's also far from them. Visits are only an hour and thirty minutes, so it would take longer to get here than the visit. Plus, the psychiatrist said they're too young to be in the main visiting area with other patients. They would have to come at a separate time. I don't think I'll put my kids through the confusion, though it's killing me not to see them.

My aunt does live somewhat around here, so I asked her to come this evening. She's bringing me shoes and a sweatshirt. It can get quite chilly in the halls and in the dining area. My roommate is leaving tonight, so likely someone new will be in here by tomorrow. This unit seems low key, so she shouldn't be too bad.

I'm struggling with downtime. I write and do the journaling assignments. I'm reading a book about recovering from losses. I think I'll find a novel to read this weekend. I'm not really into the adult coloring books or puzzles, but I may try those activities as well. The television is on after dinner, but I'm not a big fan of the crowd. There's only one group session tonight, since there are visits, so I'll have to find something to pass the time.

CHAPTER 19:
JOY IS NOT ALWAYS HAPPINESS

The journaling assignment today was to identify 30 things that make me smile. It took me nearly the full hour. How sad is that? Earlier in the week, I knocked out a full page of worries in minutes.

I was able to complete the list including getting flowers, board games with friends, listening to my son read, seeing a hummingbird, etc. The second step was to put a "c" next to all the things on your list you have control over. Only 11 things on my list were something I could initiate myself.

Sending myself flowers didn't make me smile, getting flowers delivered to me unexpectedly does. I don't have control over that. Though I can increase my chances by maybe putting out a feeder on the porch, I can't be delighted by the view a hummingbird without it being willing to cross my path. This was a big eye-opener for me.

I decided within my own mind it wasn't happiness I was after. I needed joy in my life. Happy seemed to be out of my control and dependent on others. Yet, joy it would appear comes from a source within myself.

Joy was spending time with my family. It was chatting with friends. Joy was being kind and having humor. Joy then must be a soulful action.

Romans 15:13 "May the God of hope fill you with all joy and peace as you trust in him, so that you may overflow with hope by the power of the Holy Spirit."

CHAPTER 18: GOING THROUGH THE MOTIONS

CHAPTER 20:
CONTROL ISSUES

I am definitely feeling better today and more evened out emotionally. My anxiety isn't too bad. I did get emotional during the family dinner when patients' families could come and have lunch with them. I miss my kids so much. My mom is probably coming to visit tomorrow. I've called my brother daily just to check in. He's been supportive and even said I sounded better today.

I only brought three changes of clothes, so I had to do laundry today. Honestly, it has been nice not to worry about doing my hair or make-up. There is supposed to be a movie and popcorn tonight, so we'll see how that goes. I'm trying desperately not to overeat. Snacks are everywhere! Ugh. Desserts are offered at each meal and I have been avoiding them like the plague. They have those crustless peanut butter and jelly sandwiches on the unit which are delicious. I'll admit to having had a few of those.

At first, I didn't like being around all these people. But we're all on a journey to recovery and everyone is supportive of each other. We're strangers, but here we are connected. It's nice. I'm almost afraid to go home to be alone. It's supposed to be different. I'm supposed to have new skills to use in managing my stress, anxiety, and depression. However, I've missed so much. Life goes on without you. Work, family, and friends will have all these questions and even frustrations. I don't really know how to plan to handle all of it.

~ ~ ~

I've gotten into a routine here. I like structure and having an agenda. However, I'm thinking this lack of flexibility isn't healthy. Overall, I've found I'm very rigid. I'm in or out, up or down, and no in between. Balance is key, but I just don't have it right now.

I used to think I liked staying busy, but I'm starting to see it's my way of avoiding other areas of my life. If my personal life is going bad, I overfocus on work. If work is too much, I overfocus on my social life. If I don't like the social stuff and it stresses me out, I overfocus on family. When all these areas are a source of stress, I crumble inwardly.

I'm thinking I've been overreactive to the external. Internally, especially spiritually, I'm neglectful. I have to find a way to be okay by myself. This is hard to process because I've always considered myself an independent person.

I will admit I have control issues. This is absolutely a false sense of security. If you really look around and think about all the aspects of your life, many things we just don't have control over. I have no control over other people. I have no control over people entering my life. You can kind of choose your level of contact. To some degree, you can choose if people stay, but most times you have no control over who leaves. People die. People move. People cheat. People change jobs. People get married. People go to prison. I have no control over any of that. Thinking and believing I do is irrational.

Thinking I have control creates a constant feeling of loss. I internalize and think what's wrong with me that people don't stay. This too is irrational thinking. Other people's actions are not a reflection of my character. It's my choice to feel the loss. If I were more flexible, those relationships would or could just change instead of disappear. No longer in or out of my life,

I could just change the activities we do together or the way we communicate.

CHAPTER 20: CONTROL ISSUES

CHAPTER 21:
FEELINGS ARE NOT TRUTH

Well, today is the day. I'm discharging this afternoon. I'm a little nervous to go home alone. However, I should be able to see the boys this evening; I'm so excited about that. Tomorrow, I start a partial hospital program. For the next 10 days or so, I'll come to the hospital from 9am to 3pm for outpatient therapy. It seems like a good plan to allow me to transition back to the "real world."

~ ~ ~

Chaplain had a group this morning on spirituality. It was focused on how to recognize our value.

Chaplain described the journey of life as a mountain. Everyone is struggling on some level somewhere on the mountain. While mountain climbing, we often ask "Where is God?" Even King David, who wrote most of the Book of Psalms, asked this question. In Psalm 22:1-2 King David writes, "My God, my God, why have you forsaken me? Why are you so far from saving me, so far from my cries of anguish? My God, I cry out by day, but you do not answer, by night, but I find no rest."

Why did God let this happen to me? Believe that God doesn't leave us in this place of despair and agony. Everyone is broken, no one is fully whole or complete. However, God's love can fill us, give us strength, and make us whole. He loves us deeply, perfectly, and unconditionally.

People think, if I do well, then God will love me. This isn't true. Romans 5:8 "But God demonstrates his own love for us in this: While we were still sinners, Christ died for us."

Our value is determined by the price He is willing to pay. God sees us as the most valuable thing in the world. How do we know our worth? John 3:16 "For God so loved the world that he gave his one and only Son, that whoever believes in him shall not perish, but have eternal life."

What if you don't feel valuable or feel loved? Feelings are not truth. God is truth and he is wisdom. If we lead with wisdom, then feelings will eventually follow. If you feel worthless, repeat over and over the truth that God says you are the most valuable thing on earth. The feelings will follow. If you feel unloved, repeat over and over the truth that God loves you unconditionally. The feelings will follow.

CHAPTER 22:
SHAKE IT OFF

I was at the first day of intensive outpatient treatment. I was a nervous wreck with my heart in my throat. I couldn't catch my breath, so I asked to speak with the nurse. My blood pressure was sky high, and I had a low-grade fever. I couldn't believe I forgot to take my morning medication. First day out of the hospital, and I already screwed up... Breathe.

Group leader was helpful in redirecting. You must care for your mind as you care for your body. If you broke your leg, you wouldn't say, "Oh it's all in your leg; shake it off." So, don't say, "It's all in your head; shake it off."

A daily sheet is posted in the lobby. It has the date, lunch menu, small article discussing a coping skill, and a quote for the day. The sheet for today is significant as the quote of the day is the same quote my mother gave me in a card for graduation.

"Our deepest fear is not that we are inadequate. Our deepest fear is that we are powerful beyond measure. It is our light, not our darkness that most frightens us. We ask ourselves, 'Who am I to be brilliant, gorgeous, talented, fabulous?' Actually, who are you not to be? You are a child of God. Your playing small does not serve the world. There is nothing enlightened about shrinking so that other people won't feel insecure around you. We are all meant to shine, as children do. We were born to make manifest the glory of God that is within us. It's not just in some of us; it's in everyone. And as we let our own light shine, we unconsciously give other people permission to do the same. As we are liberated from our own fear, our presence automatically liberates others." —Marianne Williamson

The quote has always spoken well to my heart and given me courage. I am a child of God. I am meant to shine. If I can ask for help and I can get well, then maybe it will give others permission to do so also.

CHAPTER 23:
FORGIVE FIRST, FEEL LATER

In group today, there was discussion about trying to do everything right and the stress it causes. And then… A God moment. Someone expressed, "I am doing everything I am supposed to do. Attending church and asking for forgiveness." However, life wasn't getting better. Then another group member said something incredibly insightful. It was suggested to turn life toward gratitude instead of getting. In prayer, instead of asking for forgiveness, because Jesus already died on the cross for you, say "thank you for forgiving me."

Why is this a God moment? The next group was spirituality and the Chaplain spoke about forgiveness. Chaplain explained forgiveness as a choice, not a feeling. If you make the choice to forgive, then the feeling will follow. If you forgive the thing, behavior, person, etc., then the hurtful feelings will lose their grip on you.

Also important is recognizing that forgiveness is not justifying behavior. If it's not okay, it's not okay. Recognize the wrong and address it with compassion and mercy. "Be kind and compassionate to one another, forgiving each other, just as in Christ God forgave you" (Ephesians 4:32).

Forgiveness has nothing to do with the other person's response. You have no control over the recipient of your forgiveness. You only have control over yourself. Unforgiveness only harbors resentment, which has no consequence for the offender. Malachy McCourt states "Resentment is like taking poison and waiting for the other person to die." Bitterness brings destruction in your life. "Get rid of all bitterness, rage and anger, brawling and slander, along with every form of malice" (Ephesians 4:31).

Forgiveness also has nothing to do with trust. "It is better to take refuge in the Lord than to trust in humans" (Psalm 118:8). See reality as what it is, not as you want it to be. There are many things we don't understand. Why did this happen to me? How could someone treat me this way? Can I ever trust this person again? There are many things we don't understand. However, forgiveness at its core is a sacrifice. "Trust in the Lord with all your heart and lean not on your own understanding; in all your ways submit to him, and he will make your paths straight" Proverbs 3:5-6).

The very act of forgiving can change your life. It can free you of resentment and bitterness and bring back joy and peace. You have the power of choice. If you choose forgiveness, then the feelings of joy and peace will follow.

CHAPTER 24:
TO DESPAIR IS HUMAN

Quote of the day: "Hope can be a powerful force. Maybe there's no actual magic in it, but when you know what you hope for most and hold it like a light within you, you can make things happen, almost like magic." —Laini Taylor

Change is so hard. For some, showing up to groups every day is a life or death decision. You can either stay in the darkness or take a step toward the light. In moving forward, you'll see that not everyone in your life will move forward with you. An internal change is happening, and others won't see it unless you show them. This transparency is hard, and you'll feel vulnerable and, at times, scared. You'll feel lonely at times as others fall away from your life as you continue to change and move in a new direction.

"Be strong and courageous. Do not be afraid; do not be discouraged, for the Lord your God will be with you wherever you go" (Joshua 1:9).

Today, though, I don't feel courageous or encouraged. I'm tired and overwhelmed with doubt. It's so hard to share my story with anyone. I'm "that person," the one folks listen to and think to themselves, *Wow, my life isn't so bad.* I don't blame them. If I looked at my own life, outside looking in, I'd feel sorry for me too.

The stress is insurmountable. In my mind, it comes and goes in seemingly manageable pieces. Write them down and it's overwhelming. Read them aloud and the fear is real. It's too much and I'm exhausted. Why am I here at all?

Your anguish isn't unique. It's an emotional trap to feel your circumstances are unparalleled. To despair is to be human. King David wrote in Psalm 55, "My thoughts trouble me and I am distraught… My heart is in anguish within me; the terrors of death have fallen on me. Fear and trembling have beset me." Your desperate reaching for relief is shared as well. "Oh, that I had the wings of a dove! I would fly away and be at rest" (Psalm 55:6).

To despair is not a sin. It's not due to a lack of belief. Jesus, prior to being arrested and crucified, experienced these intense feelings. Jesus was described as "sorrowful and troubled". Furthermore, Jesus expresses his anguish, "My soul is overwhelmed with sorrow to the point of death" (Matthew 26:36-38).

Many folks lean on Philippians 4:13 "I can do all things through Christ who gives me strength." This is absolutely true. However, to ask God to take away your troubles, is not a lack of faith. Jesus was a gift to mankind and sent here to save us all from death. He knew his purpose and was sinless giving not into temptation or the weaknesses of the flesh. Jesus falls with his face to the ground and prayed, "My Father, if it is possible, may this cup be taken from me" (Matthew 26:39). Another account of this event is in Luke 22:44 where it further describes Jesus "being in anguish, he prayed more earnestly, and his sweat was like drops of blood falling to the ground."

Feel the feelings and understand you are human and will feel despair. Also recognize Jesus shows us how to manage our troubles. He prayed and prayed. Jesus turned to his Father for strength and didn't fall into temptation. Jesus concludes his prayer outlined in Luke 22:42 with "not my will, but yours be done."

"For I know the plans I have for you, declares the Lord, plans to prosper you and not to harm you, plans to give you hope and a future. Then you will seek me and come and pray to me, and I will listen to you. You will seek me and find me when you seek me with all your heart" (Jeremiah 29:11-13).

Chapter 24: To Despair Is Human

CHAPTER 25:
IF THIS, THEN THAT

Quote of the day: "It is impossible to live without failing at something, unless you live so cautiously that you might as well not have lived at all—in which case, you fail by default." —J.K. Rowling

I knew a "what if" world was a dangerous place to live. What if my dad hadn't died? What if my mom didn't get cancer? What if I had stayed? What if I had walked out? I accepted my life "as is." I can't do anything about the past. No regrets. It is what it is.

However, I did not realize how devastating a world of "if/then" could be. Because of my past, I have this belief I can predict the future. After all the best predictor of future behavior is past behavior. I know that *if* this type of situation happens, *then* my response will be this. Why? Because I know me. I've seen me do it. *If* the situation were worse than past experiences, *then* I would collapse internally. Inpatient psychiatric care would be the only solution.

Yet, here I am having had this experience. Nothing that has happened hasn't been the same or worse. Maybe issues weren't resolved; therefore, they snowballed into something bigger. Or the danger was in thinking there's always something worse up ahead. I live in fear of the next worse, devastating thing.

God knows your heart and understands your fears. "Have no fear of sudden disaster or of the ruin that overtakes the wicked, for the Lord will be at your side and will keep your foot from being snared" (Proverbs 3:25-26).

Reinhold Neibuhr wrote probably one of the most popular prayers in modern culture, The Serenity Prayer: Accept what you can't change and change what you can. He asks for wisdom in knowing what to act on and what to accept. I cannot change all the loss I have experienced, but I can process my grief and accept a new vision of my future.

You can make a list as we did. In one column, write "act" and list all the things you can change. In the next column, write "accept" and list everything you cannot change. Pray for wisdom and let God lead you.

CHAPTER 26:
TRUTH BOMB DROPS HARD

Quote of the day: "Some people believe holding on and hanging in there are signs of great strength. However, there are times when it takes much more strength to know when to let go and then do it." —Ann Landers

Journaling assignment: How have you validated your work in treatment thus far? How have others validated or invalidated your work in treatment? AND How do you change that?

I laid the truth bomb this morning, and said out loud, that if I couldn't find a way to afford treatment then others were going to have to find a way to afford my funeral. Thinking back, I believe this was the first time I acknowledged how close to death I really came. I hadn't said it to anyone. The only other time I acknowledge this was in review of my diagnosis sheet. "Suicidal ideation with multiple plans." Then I remember the reaction I got with the nurse as she read it out loud, "*multiple* plans, oh."

I get it now how dangerous it was. I knew I needed help, that something wasn't right. However, I didn't fully grasp at that time the necessity. I needed to be here. I have to be here to even have a chance to accept my life as it is, not as I want it to be. I was ill-equipped. But I'm trying and improving. I believe I can get there. People I've told about my attempt, hospitalization, and treatment have said they were proud of me. They complimented my strength for reaching out for help. I don't feel strong, but the words are helpful, supportive, and kind. I need to believe I deserve to get better.

"Whenever you feel unloved, unimportant, or insecure, remember to whom you belong" Song of Songs 4:7)

So often we are led by our feelings, but feelings cannot be trusted. Wisdom and truth are better leaders. You may feel lost, helpless, or worthless. At times, you feel God is angry at or disappointed in you. The truth is that God has a pleasing will for you.

"Do not conform to the pattern of this world but be transformed by the renewing of your mind. Then you will be able to test and approve what God's will is - his good, pleasing and perfect will" (Romans 12:2).

CHAPTER 27:
WHAT GOD OWES US

Pastor spoke this Sunday on God's greatness from Romans 11:33 – 12:2. God is inexhaustible and with immeasurable power and He owes us... his creation... NOTHING. Take out a blank piece of paper. Number it down the side of the page. There, my friend, is a comprehensive list of everything God owes you... NOT ONE THING.

How many times have we cursed the heavens and questioned our Creator? Why did you do this, why didn't you do that, or where were you? Who in hell do you think you are? The audacity, huh?

God receives glory as He uses his greatness to love people, his creation. We owe God. We owe Him our faithfulness. We owe Him our spirit. We owe Him our love. We owe Him our lives. "But because of his great love for us, God, who is rich in mercy, made us alive with Christ even when we were dead in transgressions; it is by grace you have been saved" (Ephesians 2:4-5).

How do you show your powerful Creator love? *You bring Him glory.* "So whether you eat or drink or whatever you do, do it all for the glory of God" (1 Corinthians 10:31).

How do you bring Him glory?

- Do good. Matthew 5:16 "let your light shine before others, that they may see your good deeds and glorify your Father in heaven."
- Obey Him. John 14:15 "If you love me, keep my commands."
- Believe and have faith. Hebrews 11:6 "And without faith it is impossible to please God, because anyone who comes to him must believe that he exists and that he rewards those who earnestly seek him."

Think now; are you asking or are you doing? Are you questioning His perfect plan? Or Are you giving God glory and faithfully following him?

CHAPTER 28:
PEOPLE SUCK

Quote of the day: "There are only two ways to live your life. One is as if nothing is a miracle. The other is as though everything is a miracle." — Albert Einstein

Journaling: Does fear fit the facts?

1.   Is there something you need to change but you're allowing fear to hold you back?

I need to change my relationships and friendships. It is hard to trust and hard to be vulnerable. Boundaries are important and acknowledging there are different boundaries needed for each people in your life. Discretion is key to protecting yourself. Risking to gain is risking to lose. But there's no good without the bad. Jesus had his disciples he considered friends. Their company he sought out and they loved him. It was his friends who disowned him, lied on him, and betrayed him. But he loved them (John 21:7) and called them his brothers (Matthew 28:10).

2.   What is the cost of allowing fear to keep you from making the change?

Change is hard and requires a level of vulnerability. I could get hurt. People suck, and they can't be trusted. You risk rejection and there is brokenness in not being good enough. However, the most wonderful feelings of love have come from letting people be a part of my life. The benefits outweigh the risks. Loneliness is fear winning and consuming my life.

"So do not fear, for I am with you; do not be dismayed, for I am your God. I will strengthen you and help you; I will uphold you with my righteous right hand" (Isaiah 41:10).

Cinderella walked on broken glass

Sleeping Beauty let a whole lifetime pass

Belle fell in love with a hideous beast

Jasmine married a common thief

Ariel walked on land for love and life

Snow White barely escaped a knife

It was all about blood, sweat and tears

Because love means facing your biggest fears.

—By my friend, Julie, during treatment

CHAPTER 29:
CHALLENGE ACCEPTED

Quote of the day: "Difficulties and adversities viciously force all their might on us and cause us to fall apart, but they are necessary elements of individual growth and reveal our true potential. We've got to endure and overcome them, and move forward. Never lose hope. Storms make people stronger and never last forever." —Roy T. Bennett

It's the last day of intensive outpatient treatment. I was forced to talk positively about myself which can be very uncomfortable. I don't like compliments, but others have told me I'm smart and have pretty blue eyes. What are some things I'm good at? I had practiced this question for interviews, so the answers here were well rehearsed and far from hitting home.

What challenges have I overcome? Divorce… twice. Loss, abuse, moving houses and communities, debt, and family caregiving. It feels like a stretch to say I have overcome these things I continue to struggle with, but I am reminded that I'm a survivor.

I am unique. I have a fierce sense of independence. I have integrity and want to do the right things for the right reasons. "Better is a poor man who walks in his integrity than a rich man who is crooked in his ways" (Proverbs 28:6). Also, I will put in the effort as Hunter S. Thompson wrote "Anything worth doing is worth doing right."

How have I made others happy? My family was ecstatic when I had children. They were so proud of me when I graduated school. My best friend gets a kick out of it when I wish her a happy half birthday. My dog seems happy every time I walk in the door. These things do feel good and bring warmth to my heart.

"For we are his workmanship, created in Christ Jesus for good works, which God prepared beforehand, that we should walk in them" (Ephesians 2:10).

Chapter 30:
The Real Work Begins

First day of individual therapy

Post-traumatic stress syndrome. Most people experience trauma and most people react with stress, but they get better over time. I did not. I have spent months, years distressed. It has impacted every aspect of my life, including my work and home. It is hard just to get through the day.

Memories of my father's demise and eventual death haunt me daily. I have nightmares, flashbacks, and in my own mind I relive the event over and over. It seems the littlest things like the smell of chapstick, a Christmas ornament, or a bowl of bran flakes trigger a memory. I also encounter big triggers such as passing a car wreck on the side of the road, seeing a patient on life support, and having to talk to a family about signing a "do not resuscitate" order. I walk around on eggshells just waiting for the next bad thing to happen. Crowds feel dangerous and overwhelming.

I remember the first time I saw this car insurance commercial. It was shot as if you were driving a car. Then from the side, the car is hit by another car. The windshield splinters, the airbag blows out, and the entire scene violently shifts. My heart stopped and stuck in my throat as tear welled up in my eyes. I cried and collapsed into myself. Was that what my father experienced? No, it was worse. His face hit the steering wheel before the airbag could deploy. The car didn't come from the side, it was head-on. It was terrifying to think about, but it was his reality.

It has been years, but I can't talk about it without crying. Relationships are so hard. Everything you gain, you stand to lose. The loss is so intensely painful, it seems best not add any more people to your life. People can't be trusted anyway, right? It certainly feels that way after being lied to, cheated on, and betrayed by those who you thought truly cared.

It's the first day of individual therapy. This is the hard work. You're asked to dig deep and rip the scabs off wounds that should have healed by now. It's time to stop bleeding, allow it to heal, and grow scars.

"I will bring health and healing… I will heal my people and will let them enjoy abundant peace and security" (Jeremiah 33:6).

CHAPTER 31:
TAKE CARE

Self-care is so important! Being good to yourself isn't selfish; it's necessary. Jesus is always the best example, so let's look at how he took care.

Take a nap! Mark 4:35-38 Jesus had been teaching by the lake all day. "When evening came, he said to his disciples, 'let us go over to the other side.'" And they left the crowd. This in itself is a great message on taking a break by getting some space from your work to take care of yourself. Then Jesus took a nap. "A furious squall came up" and where did they find him? "Jesus was in the stern, sleeping on a cushion." He had a long day, worked hard, so He took time away from others and rested.

Let someone do something nice for you. Luke 7:36-47 Jesus was invited over to dinner and after dinner he reclined at the table. A woman came to him weeping and with a jar of perfume. "She began to wet his feet with her tears. Then she wiped them with her hair, kissed them, and poured perfume on them." Jesus saw she was showing Him how much she loved him and let her care for him in this moment. So, accept that gift certificate for a pedicure or the offer to mow your lawn, and let someone love on you!

Have a good cry. Life is tough, and you're not made of cold, hard stone. "When Jesus saw her weeping, and the Jews who had come along with her also weeping, he was deeply moved in spirit and troubled... Jesus wept" (John 11:33-36). It's not weakness to cry, but a strength of the heart.

Celebrate with your friends. "I am going to celebrate the Passover with my disciples at your house" (Matthew 26:18). He was able to eat dinner, recline, and talk with the ones He loved.

Hard times may be around the corner, but don't borrow trouble from tomorrow. Let yourself be joyful with the present fellowship.

CHAPTER 32:
BE STILL

My friend, please do not give up. Do not put a permanent solution on a temporary problem. You are in pain, you are hurting, and you don't believe it will ever get better. My friend, God loves you. He weeps with you. Your pain is his pain. "The Lord himself goes before you and will be with you; he will never leave nor forsake you. Do not be afraid; do not be discouraged" (Deuteronomy 31:8).

Before you hurt yourself or someone else, be still. Give yourself time and space. Stop and pray for God to help you. "The Lord will fight for you; you need only to be still" (Exodus 14:14). When I was hurting and no longer wanted to live, I was frozen in the darkness, too afraid to move. God fought for me and got me where I needed to go for help. He can do the same for you. A hospital, crisis center, or community mental health center can help you be still and get new perspective.

Three days, please just give it three days. In Matthew 27:1-7, Judas, the one who betrayed Jesus, was wrought with guilt and despair. The same morning he turned over Jesus to the authorities, Judas tried to undo what he had done, but couldn't. He left and committed suicide.

Imagine if Judas had waited three days. He would have saw Jesus rise from the dead. Jesus, being who he is, would have forgiven him. Judas, even though he had betrayed Jesus, could have turned into one of His most amazing apostles. Judas could have stood before other sinners as a living example of God's amazing grace and forgiveness. Be still, wait at least three days, ask for help, and you too one day can stand before others as an example of God's saving grace.

"As Scripture says, 'Anyone who believes in him will never be put to shame.' For there is no difference between Jew and Gentile- the same Lord is Lord of all and richly blesses all who call on him, for, 'Everyone who calls on the name of the Lord will be saved" (Romans 10:11-13).

NOTES

NOTES

NOTES

NOTES

NOTES

NOTES

NOTES

www.ingramcontent.com/pod-product-compliance
Lightning Source LLC
Chambersburg PA
CBHW061740020426
42331CB00006B/1304